Caleb Davis Bradlee

Sermons for the Church

Caleb Davis Bradlee

Sermons for the Church

ISBN/EAN: 9783744744317

Printed in Europe, USA, Canada, Australia, Japan

Cover: Foto ©Lupo / pixelio.de

More available books at **www.hansebooks.com**

SERMONS FOR THE CHURCH

BY

CALEB DAVIS BRADLEE, D.D.

PASTOR (PRO TEM.) OF CHRIST'S CHURCH, LONGWOOD

BOSTON
GEO. H. ELLIS, 141 FRANKLIN STREET
1893

Dedicated

TO MY FRIEND OF MANY YEARS
THE HONORABLE AND JUDGE FREDERICK W. RICORD
OF NEWARK, NEW JERSEY

PREFACE.

In 1888 I gave to the public a volume of sermons, entitled "Sermons for All Sects."

This book was so kindly received, I have ventured to make another offering to those who may choose to accept the same. I have selected the title "Sermons for the Church," because I wish to speak to all of every church who are disciples of our Lord Jesus Christ.

CALEB DAVIS BRADLEE.

CONTENTS.

		PAGE
1.	HOLY GROUND,	9

"Put off thy shoes from thy feet; for the place whereon thou standest is holy ground."— ACTS vii. 33.

2. OUR MOTHERS, ... 21

"There stood by the cross of Jesus his mother."— ST. JOHN xix. 25.

3. OUR MANSIONS IN HEAVEN, ... 34

"In my Father's house are many mansions."— ST. JOHN xiv. 2.

4. MORDECAI SITTING AT THE KING'S GATE, ... 46

"All this availeth me nothing so long as I see Mordecai, the Jew, sitting at the king's gate."— ESTHER v. 13.

5. NEW THINGS, ... 56

"Some new thing."— ACTS xvii. 21.

6. CAN GOD BE DISCOVERED? 67

"Canst thou by searching find out God?"— JOB xi. 7.

7. THE FATAL SUBSTITUTE, ... 77

"Send, I pray thee, by the hand of him whom thou wilt send."— EX. iv. 13.

8. ILLUSIONS, ... 87

"What is your life? A vapor?"— ST. JAMES iv. 14.

9. THE CORONATION OF FAILURE, ... 97

"Thou shalt not go over."— DEUT. xxxiv. 4.

10. DISCONTENT, ... 109

"Oh that I had wings like a dove!"— Ps. lv. 6.

11. LOOKING TO THE FUTURE, ... 120

"I will fetch my knowledge from afar."— JOB xxxvi. 3.

CONTENTS

		PAGE
12.	TRANSIENT SIGHT OF GOD,	129
	"How little a portion is heard of him!"—JOB xxvi. 14.	
13.	TRUE CHRISTIANS,	137
	"One fold, one shepherd."—ST. JOHN x. 16.	
14.	THE EXCLUSIVE SPIRIT,	149
	"No room for them in the inn."—ST. LUKE ii. 7.	
15.	THE GLORY OF NAZARETH,	158
	"Can there any good thing come out of Nazareth?"—ST. JOHN i. 46.	
16.	THE WEDDING GARMENT,	169
	"Friend, how camest thou in hither, not having a wedding garment?"—ST. MATT. xxii. 12.	
17.	THE OMNIPRESENCE OF THE ALMIGHTY,	181
	"Not far from every one of us."—ACTS xvii. 27.	
18.	THE SOUL'S WEIGHT,	190
	"Thou art weighed in the balance, and art found wanting."—DAN. v. 27.	
19.	THE CHRISTIAN MARK,	202
	"They took knowledge of them, that they had been with Jesus."—ACTS iv. 13.	
20.	THE GRACE OF GOD,	212
	"By the grace of God, I am what I am."—1 COR. xv. 10.	
21.	PLEASANT WORDS,	222
	"Pleasant words are as an honeycomb, sweet to the soul."—PROV. xvi. 24.	
22.	SPIRITUAL CLIMBING,	232
	"O God, set me up on high."—PS. lxix. 29.	
23.	THE COMMANDS OF GOD,	243
	"Thus saith the Lord."—EX. xi. 4.	
24.	THE BREVITY OF LIFE,	256
	"Knoweth that he hath but a short time."—REV. xii. 12.	
25.	A POSTPONED CONCLUSION,	267
	"But the end is not yet."—ST. MATT. xxiv. 6.	

I.

HOLY GROUND.

"Put off thy shoes from thy feet; for the place whereon thou standest is holy ground."— ACTS vii. 33

LET us never forget, and let us always keep the fact in our minds, as a sparkling, uplifting, and celestial truth, that every place where we stand is "holy ground." Let us never rest patiently with that easy and wicked creed which, while allowing that some places are sacred, tacitly admits that there are other places where we all can do as we please. No: we can never get away from the sight of God, and we can never escape out of the region of duty.

The temple is holy; and so is the house, the street, the place of business, and every spot upon the earth.

Of course, certain localities and certain buildings, from the very fact of being especially dedicated to religion, obtain an additional sanctity, and stand out prominently as worthy of our deepest veneration. It would be but a poor philosophy in us, however, to say that, because some things are especially sacred, that all other things are profane. Everywhere the ground is holy, and in all places we must put off the shoes of anything and everything that may be flavored with weakness and wrong. All the world is the audience-chamber of Heaven; and we are living in a vast whispering-gallery, so that every breath is reported at the throne of Almighty God.

Yes, the world is all holy ground. Certainly, there is sin enough in it, sorrow enough in it, and mystery enough about it, to make us think at times but very little about its sacredness,—nay, enough to turn our eyes entirely another way,—ay, almost enough to arouse our scepticism, to stir up our misanthropy, and to bury us in the deepest gloom. But is there not also a great deal of glory that can be detected if one will only turn the eyes the right way? Are we obliged always to look on the dark side, and is it wise to endeavor to put out the sun? Look with me, if you please, at the holy side of life. It is holy because of the power of friendship that it offers. There is such a thing as true friendship; and it runs its blessed trails of light all along the relationships of life, being found often in its most benignant form in husband and wife, in parent and child, in brother and sister, in neighbor with neighbor, and in friend with friend. I am aware that there are some philosophers who will sneer at such remarks as these.

There are some who believe that all the people in the world are actuated by selfishness, who confidently assert that there is no higher motive ruling all hearts than self-seeking; but they are wofully mistaken! I do not doubt that in their own souls they are prominent illustrations of what they assert; but they should not attempt to measure all humanity from their own shrivelled, dilapidated, and empty standpoint. Tell me, O philosopher, is the wife selfish, as she watches her sick husband day after day, night after night, and week after week, until the roses fade from her cheek, the strength creeps from her limbs, and she herself falls into stillness, as the one for whom she cared gets well? I have known such a case. Is the mother selfish who gives up everything for her child, yet is so very self-forgetful as never to call it giving up? Such occurrences are very common. Ah! all around us, daily and hourly, are plenty of stirring examples of disinterested love, filling the air with a delicious aroma, and consecrating the ground where they occur.

Only with the right mind and the willing heart let us take a good look on the bright side of life, and we shall be satisfied that all souls are not soaked in a pitiable selfishness. Again, life is holy because it is a field of usefulness. There are always plenty of noble deeds waiting for our fellowship, and opportunities are constantly occurring by which we can do vast good. Never a day rolls by when we cannot, if we will, make our influence fragrant, touching, and beautiful. It is done by a smile, by a tear, by a shake of the hand, by a cup of cold water, by a genial word, and by almost anything that leaps hot from a loving heart upon a waiting, anxious, and hungry soul. All of us can, if we will, become spiritually great. Spiritual diamonds, pearls, rubies, and all sorts of precious gems are profusely scattered from

Heaven at our feet; while, if we are only clothed with a blessed, a glorious, and a happy insight, we can very easily stoop down and pick them up.

When we come to die, how sacred will be the retrospect, if we find that all our earthly pilgrimage is thoroughly perfumed with benefactions, and if we discover that we have passed our days as fountains of refreshment to all within our possible reach! Then the last breath will be sweet, the cold perspiration gathering upon the brow will be a sparkling constellation of glory, and the ascending spirit will be engirdled by a guard of rejoicing angels.

Again, life is holy because of the spiritual privileges with which it is enshrined. I am aware that there are not many who stop to think of this. I know that many of those who do think of it and acknowledge it dwell upon the fact but briefly. Yet, my friends, can anything be more sublime than this bounty of God, by which all men have souls, and souls, too, that can grow? Is it nothing that we can think, feel, and speak? Is it nothing that we can understand the names of God and Christ, and that we can realize the great truth of immortality? It appears to me that the very fact that we can worship, that we can anoint time with the grandeur of prayer, bathe it with the sobs of penitence, and swathe it with good resolutions,—this very fact is itself peculiarly sublime, strangely comforting, and sweetly sacred.

Tell me is not everything here on earth very solemn, when we consider that our stay here is so short, that events are so uncertain, and that everything is so prophetic? We are swimming on a sea of immense possibilities; and is not every ripple on its surface full of mighty suggestions that are pregnant with grandeur? Take a reverent view of the space that must be traversed, of the billows that must be mastered, and of everything that occurs on the voyage of life. Keep on the watch all the time for that which will stir the heart to gratitude, rouse it to devout wonder, and thrill it with holy joy. Travel with open eyes and listening ears, that all the time inspiration may salute the soul, making salvation sure.

Yes, even our temptations and pains, rightly viewed and righteously treated, may prove to us not a hindrance, but a gain, and may enable us to make the ground holy. Are not temptations resisted and pains nobly endured a splendid and an inspiriting sight? If you see a man or a woman, all covered over with enticements to do wrong, and solicited by every art of persuasion, yet standing firm, calm, and persistently pure, without a scar, and without a stain, perfectly clean, does not earth then appear to you something more than common, and is it not anointed with a gorgeous transfiguration, and do you not feel somehow consecrated by the beautiful sight? You see, too, a man or a woman bearing suffering patiently, keeping very radiant, very serene, and full of a vital hope, overflowing with buoyant trust, thanking God even for stripes, and christening blows with a sweet submission, as gifts disguised: does not then all about them and all near to them seem holy? Have they not anointed their very neighborhood with a celestial fragrance? Are they not so many way-marks set up upon the earth to prove to us all that heaven is not far away, nor the road thither blocked up?

Of old it was promised that five good people should save Sodom. Are there not a much larger number than this who will save and spiritualize us to-day? "Put off thy shoes." This was the command of old, because the place was consecrated, and it was not meant that anything rough should contaminate it; and it has a meaning and a warning for us this day. It means that we must give up our loose ideas of life as a game of chance, or as a spasm of mere pleasure, or as a prison-house of despair. We must not look at existence with sceptical and misanthropic eyes, as if there were no hope, no sanctity, and no brilliancy about it. We must stand within the vast cathedral of life with an august spirit of true veneration. We must hear its magnificent vesper services, as they sweep upon the air with tremendous power and with thrilling melody.

We must listen to its great organ,—the greatest that was ever built, with its wonderful *vox humana* stop, that can give us every tone ever known: then we shall become enraptured with the music as it is echoed to remotest space. Heaven's choirs are all around us, and they are chanting all the time. Can we not hear them, or are we so deaf that nothing but the resurrection trump will cause us to listen? Oh, let us open our ears, put off every obstruction, cultivate a spirit of devotion, encourage the feeling of submission, stir up the exhilarating influences of hope, understand our mighty privileges, be swathed with a consciousness of our awful responsibilities, and be dazzled, bewildered, and sanctified by the majestic thought of our future possible glory!

Life is very much what we make it; and let us make it sublime, let us lift its valleys into hills, change its hills to mountains, and raise its mountains into heaven, keeping ourselves ever upon the summit! Why need we ever get tame, discouraged, morose, and sinful? Why need we ever surround ourselves with marshy land, living in the morass, and being contented with swamps? Certainly, there is something better for us all than such things.

"Holy ground." Of course, all the land about Palestine we are quite ready to call holy ground. We all have a great desire to see the sacred places there; and a large majority of us, if we had the means and the time, would start for the East at once, would make a long stay, and would return home with many precious suggestive and holy relics. Who would not like a quiet sail on the Sea of Tiberias? Who would not wish to stand on the Mount of Transfiguration? Who would not be pleased to sleep one night in the Garden of Gethsemane? Would it not be pleasant to walk through Bethlehem, and to search out

all the familiar spots at Nazareth, and to tarry at Jerusalem awhile? Ah! these names, and others equally precious, call up many fragrant thoughts!

We feel that by the great privilege of travel we could bring Jesus near; while we are apt to consider that that distant land is, in a peculiar sense, very holy. But, my friends, to-day, if we will, Jesus can be brought very near to us; and to-day all the ground around us may be rendered sacred by his holy tread. We may have a Bethlehem, Nazareth, Jerusalem, and everything we want in our own hearts. We should become so closely allied to our Master that all Scriptural history may be somewhat enacted in our own experience; and then, and not till then, will the mission of our Lord Jesus Christ be fully carried out.

Do we talk about going to the Holy Land? Why, we are not fit to go there *till we have become holy ourselves*. The Crusaders years ago would have accomplished something if every man in their ranks had been really a disciple. If Peter the Hermit had also been Peter the saint, the visit to Jerusalem would have been with power, while now we should not find unbelievers guarding the sacred city. Reverence for localities is a good thing, but reverence for our own souls is a much better trait of character. Oh, let us not abate one jot nor one tittle our veneration for any spot that reminds us of heaven! Yet, at the same time, let us have everywhere and in all emergencies the "kingdom of heaven" within us, so that our goodness may shine more and more unto the perfect day.

Let Sunday always be kept by us in solemn regard, and the services in the sanctuary be constantly acknowledged; and let us look at the Bible as at no other book, and fulfil thoroughly all the rites of religion! But may we remember, also, that every day must be a day of worship, and that our hourly duties must be transfigured by a light from the celestial city. "The place where thou standest is holy ground." "Where *thou* standest." That is, every place where you are. There is an ancient legend something like this: A mighty giant wanted to find a power that was greater than his own, in order that he might change his habits of life, and from a ruler become a servant; and so he went to a king who was noted for his bravery, and he thought that he had found one unto whom he might with dignity submit. For a long while all things went smoothly; and the giant did mighty work for his master, both in peace and war and in sorrow and mirth, until one day the king was thrown into terrible fear by hearing a minstrel utter the name of "Satan." Then said the giant, "If 'Satan' be so great, he shall be my next ruler"; but, after serving him for a long time, they both happened to see a Cross, when the evil one trembled, and said:

> "''Twas *there* Christ Jesus died;
>   Wherever stands a cross like that,
> I may not, dare not, bide.'
> 'Ho, ho,' the giant cried again,
>   Surprised again, perplexed,
> 'Then Jesus is the greatest king:
>   I seek and serve him next.'"

So the restless one goes around the earth to find Jesus, and at last comes to a hermit's cell, who directs him to fast and pray, and then he tells him he will find what he desires. But these directions, after a short time, were not pleasant to the seeker, so the hermit says to him (and I will give the words in the poetical garb of an unknown writer from whom I have already quoted): —

"Then said the hermit, 'Giant, since
    Thou canst not fast nor pray,
I know not if our Master will
    Serve thee some other way.
But go down to yon river deep,
    Where pilgrims daily sink,
And build for thee a little hut,
    Close on the river's brink,
And carry travellers back and forth
    Across the raging stream.
Perchance this service to our King
    A worthy one will seem.'
For many a year, in lowly hut,
    The giant dwelt content
Upon the bank, and back and forth
    Across the stream he went,
And on his giant shoulders bore
    All travellers who came
By night, by day, or rich or poor,
    All in King Jesus' name:
But much he doubted if the King
    His work would note or know,
And often with a weary heart
    He waded to and fro.
One night, as wrapped in sleep he lay,
    He sudden heard a call,

'O mighty giant, come carry me!'
Down on the bank a little child
    He found, a piteous sight,
Who, weeping, earnestly implored
    To cross that very night.
With gruff good will he picked him up,
    And on his neck to ride
He tossed him, as men play with babes,
    And plunged into the tide;
But, as the water closed around
    His knees, the infant's weight
Grew heavier and heavier
    Until it was so great
The giant scarce could stand upright,
    His staff shook in his hand,
His mighty knees bent under him,
    He barely reached the land,
And, staggering, set the infant down,
    And turned to scan his face,
When, lo! he saw a halo bright,
    Which lit up all the place;
And then the giant fell down, afraid
    At marvel of the thing,
And dreamed not that it was the face
    Of Jesus Christ, his King,
Until the infant spoke and said,
    'O mighty one, behold!
I am the Lord, whom thou hast served:
    Rise up, be glad, and bold.'"

This legend strikingly teaches us that, when we do our duty, we are on holy ground, that service to our fellow-creatures illuminates and sanctifies every spot that we tread, and that even the cup of cold water given in the name of a disciple changes earth to heaven.

"Put off thy shoes." We all know what it is that we have to put off before we are fit to stand where we are. The weakness is different with each one of us, but very powerful with all of us. A great deal depends upon our education, our habits, our circumstances, our transmitted tendencies, and our vacillating or toughened will. But, whether our sin be little or great, be natural or inherited, be tightly hold of us or joined to the soul by a frail thread, we must resolutely, believingly, and thoroughly *put it off*. Let there be no compromise, no dallying, no soft words, and no murmured excuses! Let us put it off with a toss or with a wrench, no matter which, as long as it goes: then each of us can stand up a man or a woman or a child on consecrated ground!

Then we shall be all ready to stand up without trembling, as the trumpet shall call us into the New Jerusalem, where we shall never regret any sacrifice that we have made by which the heart became better and by which the whole inner life was transfigured.

So doing, our welcome will be very sure, comforting, and hearty.

II.

OUR MOTHERS.

"There stood by the cross of Jesus his mother." — ST. JOHN xix. 25.

WHO better could be selected as the witness of that last terrible agony than the Master's mother? At such an hour he needed one who was so very near and so very dear. Yet would it not have been better, had she kept away? How could she endure such a sight? It was her son that was covered with such a temporary shame and filled with such awful pangs. You know, in the engraving that represents the scene, she is supported from almost the faintness of death by some of the other female disciples. Poor woman! Her heart was broken, as well it might be, under such a load as that. *Why was she there?* Mary, I do you dishonor by such a question! Mothers of the race, I impeach your devotion by the mere supposition of her absence! Where else could that gentle parent be than where the loved one was pouring out his life? Keep away? *That was not possible.* She must look on, although the nerves snap, one by one, while numbness creeps silently over the whole frame. She must be present, although every nail driven breaks a cord of the heart, and although she be worse than crucified herself by the sight of the torture. As we carry ourselves back and stand at the cross, we involuntarily cry out, "God pity and help that mother!"

I would speak to-day of our mothers, *Heaven bless them!* If they are faithful, their names are wreathed around the soul, and are written in bright and glorious letters in the Book of God. The nearest friend that we have on earth and in heaven, God and Christ, of course, being excepted, is our mother. I speak this with caution, and out of a solemn conviction. I know that there is another relation, tender, true, sacred, close, and beautiful; but no other tie can wipe out nor tarnish in the least nor remove one iota the obligations of our birth, while he or she who, because they are married, forget the head of their early home, must sooner or later *pay a heavy penalty for the sin.* Of course, the relations of a man or a woman to their early home alter with each advancing year, beginning at first with implicit obedience, and then growing into respect, affection, and service. Among true Christians there will be no clashing of interests, since both sides and all sides will readily understand their respective positions, and will claim no more than their due share of attention, while the name "mother-in-law" will cease to be repulsive. I claim, then, for the first place in your heart your mother,— first, because *placed there first,* because she has sacrificed so much in order to earn that position, and because you yourselves wish to secure just that stand in the affection of your own children. I say that she has earned the right of the highest place in your regard, and I challenge a denial! How many sleepless nights and anxious days she has undergone for our sakes! How readily she has sacrificed all social pleasures that the little ones in the house might not be neglected! How nimbly her fingers have worked, in order that she might obtain the necessary clothing for each season, as it rapidly rolled around!

How patiently she has watched the growing child, gazing intently at each look and each movement, and examining each tone and each breath, in order to ascertain if all things run smoothly and well! How frequently she has retired to her chamber that she might quietly pray for the lambs, thus gaining the right spirit, by the power of which she could properly train their young souls! How careful she has been of her own expenses, so as to have a large margin by which she may get comforts for the little ones, such as she feels they so much need! How kindly she listens to all the trials that come up, yielding her smiles or her tears or her gentle rebukes, as occasion requires! How often she overlooks a great deal because she knows that it is not worth while to be all the time finding fault, and because she is wise enough to understand that a great deal of naughtiness is simply an excess of animal life, which must not be tamed too much! What constant lessons she gives of carefulness, politeness, honesty, good nature, and religion! She has taught the children how to pray; and often, too, she has prayed with them. She has become acquainted with all the teachers of her dear ones, showing an interest both in their Sunday and secular instruction. She has made herself acquainted with all the companions and playmates of the household, weeding out such as were unworthy.

As the boys or girls have come forward into manhood or womanhood, she has stood by them as counsellor and friend; and, when they have married, she has welcomed the new comer for their sakes, writing his or her name upon her heart,—that most difficult task of all. So on, through all their changes, she has stood sentinel, until at last, her work done, God calls her away; and then the memory of her is fragrant from generation to generation, as her children and her children's children rise up and call her blessed.

Of course, sisters in Christ, I have spoken of the good mother, such as I hope you have all possessed, and such as I hope that every one who is named mother will become. Let me now address myself to mothers, with some suggestions and recapitulations of their duties. First, think of the responsible office that you fill. We hear every day of "woman's rights"; and they have rights such as they do not now possess, and such as they will in time receive, and may God hasten the blessed day! But I know of no rights more grand, more lofty, more sacred, more sublime, more far-reaching, more deep, more rich, and more eternal than the right, the privilege, and the glory of educating souls. You want to step into the pulpit, you want to plead at the bar, you want to officiate in surgery, and you want to be merchants. Well, let such as are able go that way; but you may be all these, and yet not step out of the beautiful privacy of your own homes.

Train up your sons, by nature or by adoption, to walk in these ways, and then will you move the world. Ay, you do move the world; and what more do you want? It is your mind and your heart that are written on the brows and the lips of every orator, every statesman, every scholar, and every great man that ever lived.

Think, then, as you deal with the children, of the majestic power that rests in your hands! You are touching the keys of the world's great organ, while you must do so, as a spiritual artist, so that the music shall be very sweet, uplifting, and pure. Again, remember that these souls are not only to play their little part in this earthly kingdom that is so transitory, but bear in mind that they are to last forever, and remember they are to become citizens of the spirit-world. Then will you not only teach them lessons of worldly prudence, such as courtesy, forbearance, generosity, studiousness, carefulness, sobriety, activity, and tact, but also will you add instruction concerning God, Christ, and eternity, with the obligations of every human being in reference to these great realities. I like to insist upon this point, because there are so many who think it but of little account, and so many, too, who neglect it altogether. You know how apt many are to commend *success* rather than character, *brightness* rather than goodness, *politeness* rather than purity, *shrewdness* rather than philanthropy, *intellect* rather than heart, and *caution* rather than honesty. How many say, Make a great man or woman, make a brilliant match, aim at an enviable notoriety, strive to be clothed in purple and fine linen, and endeavor by all means to enter the first circles, instead of saying, First of all be true, be pure, and be holy: then, if prosperity be yours, very well, and, if not, quite as well! Keep a clear conscience, and then leave results.

As your children enter into the marriage state, be resolved that their partners shall respect and love you, whether they wish to do so or not, and make it a certain thing that your gentleness shall thaw their icy hearts, although they may be frozen all up into solid lumps. If it takes years to bring about what you wish, still work on, in faith, love, and prayer; for the thaw will surely come. I have seen case after case where both parties — mother-in-law and daughter-in-law — were excellent people, — ay, in many cases, superior people, but where, by some strange coincidence, a terrible clashing has come. The fault is often wholly on one side, but perhaps more often on both sides. Of course, there must be a great deal of giving up, while one side must give up a great deal more than the other. The trial is certainly greater to you, mothers. You have brought up your sons or your daughters in a way that you deemed just and right: you have educated them to the best of your ability, and certain habits you have taught them that have appeared to you proper, equitable, respectful, and holy. Now another party steps into your place, who is very apt to call in question your whole management, and perhaps is quite apt to say that your tuition has been a failure simply because that other party was brought up in a different way.

Well, how can it be helped? When you were married, you probably did the same thing, although you have now forgotten it, or, if you did not *say* anything, you undoubtedly kept up a tremendous amount of thinking; or, if you are wholly innocent either of speaking or thinking such unpleasant things, then you are just that sort of person who deserves to have the praise and the admiration of all the holy on the earth and in heaven! Try in every way to keep down this friction that is so unpleasant; and, if the other side will not pour their oil into the rough places, then take a good supply out of the canister of your own soul, and throw it on, and keep throwing it on, until the wheels all work smoothly and gracefully. Then will you have gained, instead of losing, a child. I know that I am asking a great deal of you; but it is my duty in this, as in every case, to take the highest Christian standpoint, and to urge you up to the very topmost peak of righteousness. If you cannot reach the summit, go as far as you can. Never put an end to your acts of kindness to your children because they have gone away and have found another home. Let them know that the old ark is always open for their visits, and for the coming of all who are dear to them. Bless them often by gifts of your own handiwork. You know best of all what they most need and like. Surprise them often with little comforts, with delicacies for the table, and with some article of clothing not easily purchased. Many a man and many a woman will show you with pride anything that their mother made. Everything that comes from the early home is worth twice as much from that very fact. Do not cease to pray for your offspring because you no longer kneel at their side and no longer hold their little hands. Pray for them? Yes, they need it all the more now that they are away from your fostering care. For often the clouds lower and the thunder rattles and the lightning gleams, while life itself is wreathed in darkness. Your prayers will give them courage, hope, peace, faith, and joy; and then they can stand up to their post with a holy serenity and with a lofty enthusiasm. They can stand there without a tear and without a frown, when they know that they are gloriously panoplied by your daily intercessions.

If, in the course of Providence, you are called to survive those who by the course of nature would seem to be ordained as your survivors, provided it be possible, be with them when they die. Then no face will they crave so much as yours. They will want your last kiss and the pressure of your hand, as they ascend to God. If you are not present at such a time, they will go away into the new country very lonely. You have been so closely connected with them from their birth that, as they are about to enter the new birth, they will want your holy encouragement and your beautiful benediction. Keep your departed children ever green in your memories. Do not strive, as some do, to drive the thought of them away, as an intrusion and as an affliction.

I would not have you mourn all the time, wearing a gloomy look and acting as if you did not believe in the other and the better life. No, never. But let the departed somehow be around you and with you, as "guardian angels," if you will, so that all loneliness shall be gone, so that somehow, in a new and in a very bright sense, on this side, the dead shall be alive. Thus will your influence over those who remain become more sweet, and thus will your example over all that you know be made powerful for good.

Sisters in Christ, are you good mothers? There is a great deal of discussion to-day about family government. "Young America," it is said, is running away with us. The order of many homes is anything but what it should be. Parents and children have sometimes changed places, while the sceptre is wielded by tiny hands. "Woe unto a nation whose king is a child!" Woe unto the house whose monarch is a boy or a girl!

How is it, my friends, with us? Do we find it very hard to say no? Has it become a very easy and a very fatal habit with us, in order that we may save ourselves from annoyance, to say yes to every whim of the children? If such be the case, then the future is indeed dark for us, while we have good reason for dreading an earthquake in our own dominions. Of course, we must say yes a great many times, and some of us much more frequently than we do; but there are times when all of us must say no, and must say it right in the face of teasing, fretting, crying, and all opposition whatsoever. Else the future of our offspring will be very apt to be either sickness and a grave or shame and a jail.

"There stood by the cross of Jesus his mother." Let that mother be the model for the mothers of all time! Study her history, as far as the New Testament gives it; and then you will be surprised at the many splendid traits that are suggested and revealed. Although we cannot think it right that we should make Mary an object of direct worship, we all of us, I know, the more we become acquainted with her character, will be willing to hold her in the highest regard, will love to speak of her with the most tender interest, and will try to follow in her steps as far as God shall give us grace. Mother! Thanks be to God that he has given us that name! I would ever speak it with a sweet tenderness and with a holy reverence. I would wear it as a celestial jewel upon my heart, and as one of the best gifts of the good Father. I would lift it up with many choice blessings, as I hold my secret intercourse with the Eternal One.

Oh, may all understand the fragrance that is wrapped up in the title, the glory that engirdles the relationship, and all the power, all the beauty, and all the grandeur that sweeten and hallow the circle of its blessed influence!

A friend one day placed in my hand a beautiful piece of poetry, entitled "My Mother at the Gate." The author I do not know; but the sweet spirit that pervades the whole of it let us all cordially acknowledge: —

"Oh, there's many a lovely picture
   On memory's silent wall,
There's many a cherished image
   That I tenderly recall!
That sweet home of my childhood,
   With its singing brooks and birds;
The friends who grew beside me,
   With their loving looks and words;
The flowers that decked the wildwood,
   The roses fresh and sweet,
The blue-bells and the daisies
   That blossomed at my feet,—
All, all are very precious,
   And often come to me,
Like the breezes from a better land,
   Beyond life's troubled sea.
But the sweetest, dearest picture
   That memory can create
Is the image of my mother,
   My mother at the gate.

"It is there I see her standing,
   With her face so pure and fair,
With the sunlight and the shadows
   On her snowy cap and hair.

　　　　I can feel the soft, warm pressure
　　　　　　Of the hand that clasped my own;
　　　　I can see the look of fondness
　　　　　　That in her blue eyes shone;
　　　　I can hear her parting blessing
　　　　　　Through the lapse of weary years;
　　　　I can see, through all my sorrows,
　　　　　　Her own sweet, silent tears.
　　　　Ah! amid the darkest trials
　　　　　　That have mingled with my fate,
　　　　I have turned to that dear image,
　　　　　　My mother at the gate.

　　　"But she has crossed the river,
　　　　　She is with the angels now,
　　　She has laid aside earth's crosses,
　　　　　And the crown is on her brow.
　　　She is clothed in clean white linen,
　　　　　And she walks the streets of gold.
　　　O loved one, safe forever
　　　　　Within the Saviour's fold,
　　　No sorrowing thoughts can reach thee,
　　　　　No grief is thine to-day.
　　　God gives thee joy for mourning,
　　　　　Thy tears are wiped away!
　　　Thou art waiting in that city
　　　　　Where the saints and angels wait,
　　　And I'll know thee, dearest mother,
　　　　　When I reach the pearly gate!"

NOTES.

"What is wanting," said Napoleon one day to Madame Campan, "in order that the youth of France be well educated?" "Good mothers," was the reply. The emperor was most forcibly struck with this answer. "Here," said he, "is a system in one word." *Abbott.* (*Ballou.*)

"If there be aught surpassing human deed or word or thought, it is a mother's love."—*Marchioness de Spadura.* (*Ballou.*)

"The future destiny of the child is always the work of the mother."—*Napoleon.* (*Ballou.*)

"Youth fades, love droops, the leaves of friendship fall: a mother's secret hope outlives them all."— *Holmes.* (*Ballou.*)

"An ounce of mother," says the Spanish proverb, "is worth a pound of clergy."— *T. W. Higginson.* (*Ballou.*)

"Stories first heard at a mother's knee are never wholly forgotten,— a little spring that never quite dries up in our journey through scorching years."— *Raffini.* (*Ballou.*)

"Even He that died for us upon the cross, in the last hour, in the unutterable agony of death, was mindful of his mother, as if to teach us that this holy love should be our last worldly thought,— the last point of earth from which the soul should take its flight for heaven."—*Longfellow.* (*Ballou.*)

"Maternal love! thou word that seems all bliss." *Pollok.* (*Ballou.*)

III.

OUR MANSIONS IN HEAVEN.

"In my Father's house are many mansions."—St. John xiv. 2.

THANKS be to Almighty God for that blessed assurance that is given to us by the holy Lord that in heaven there are many mansions! We could not all of us live together in one house on the earth, however large the house; nor will it be well for us to do so in the Celestial City, at least right away, and just as we are when we leave the tabernacle of clay.

Then, again, I know no reason why the family circle should be entirely broken at death, nor why we cannot have our little special circles above as well as here on the earth.

Of course, in the spiritual world everything that savors of exclusiveness, pride, and ambition will be forever banished. If you would have a better locality there than I have, your main desire will be to lift me up to your level. Then, again, we shall all know each other there, love each other, and work for each other in all good ways; while jealousy, ill will, and criticism will be unknown. The affinities of heaven may perhaps be divided into three ascending stages: first, the attractions of families and kindred; secondly, the fellowship of mental powers; but, lastly, and best of all, the communion of progressive souls. I love to think of an unbroken family circle in God's holy city. Even the totally depraved cannot be always shut out from the ministrations of those who on earth were the nearest and the dearest; but certainly those who have tried to do their duty while in the flesh must, in the city of the New Jerusalem, be in the closest bonds of a beautiful communion.

The idea which prevails so extensively in some classes of minds that in eternity we are all thrown together in one promiscuous crowd all the time, with our special relationship entirely and thoroughly ignored, appears to be absurd, unreasonable, and undevout.

That we shall, as saints, on certain occasions assemble together for the praise of God and the Lamb, I do not doubt. Nay, it would be very strange indeed if we did not have our harps in our hands and our songs upon our lips very frequently; but that this should be all that we do would be equally strange and terribly sad. No, there, without any doubt, will be our own mansion. It will be marked with our own name, and it will be sacred to our own dear ones, where we can spend many private hours in a goodly, happy, and glorious fellowship. Were this not the case, our homes here would be a mockery,— yes, a terrible and a strange delusion.

What a satire upon the dearest spot on the earth, if we maintain that it is only bounded by breath, and if we assert that there must at last, and that very briefly, be thrown an awful pall upon its mighty possibilities,—a thick cloud upon its holy friendships, and a thorough eclipse upon its splendid culture!

Ah! can it be that husband and wife, father and mother, son and daughter, and brother and sister, mean nothing whatever save on the mortal side? We do not ask that these names shall signify the same in heaven as they do here; but have we not an undoubted reason to suppose that they will mean the same thing in a spiritualized sense? Probably one reason why death causes such a fearful chill in so many hearts as dear ones are removed is a feeling that the grave is all, or that the other life is so undefined, so shadowy, so ghost-like, and so entirely different from anything seen or known here as to be almost as good as no life whatever, or as about equivalent to non-existence. Yet state to all troubled ones that the other world is a great deal like this world, only a great deal better; that no ties of the heart are severed and no real fellowship broken; that there are houses there with vacant chambers for those not yet arrived; and that everything is real, and more real than here. Then all things are consecrated: sorrow becomes illuminated, excessive grief is dispelled, heaven attracts rather than repels, life gains in splendor, trials have their golden side, sickness wears a robe of light, and even death has its diamond experience; while the name of home becomes resplendent with power, honor, and glory.

Many are the poets that speak of home.
Goldsmith says,—

> "Such is the patriot's boast, where'er we roam
> His first, best country ever is at home."

Cotton says,—

> "The world has nothing to bestow.
> From our own selves our joys must flow,
> And that dear hut,— our home."

Payne says,—

> "'Mid pleasures and palaces though we may roam,
> Be it ever so humble, there's no place like home."

So, undoubtedly, millions of others might be quoted who speak of the benediction of home; but would they have so written, or would they have thought home a benediction, unless they believed in its perpetuity, seeing on the other side of the beautiful river only its reglorification and its sure baptism of light?

Home! Your home and my home! How different our gaze at it, as we say temporal or as we say eternal! If transient, why, then, what clouds hang over every birth, what woes cluster around every marriage vow, and how the family altar is ever draped in black!

If permanent, then every babe is an evangel from the skies, every true marriage service an anthem from heaven; while the family altar is ever festooned with flowers. Oh, can we hesitate on which side to place our faith, when one side is so dark and the other side so light; when with one view our true identity is but of brief continuance, while by the other prospect all heaven is studded with peaceful homes and loving hearts, like as some bright night you see the whole firmament paved with stars?

And with this joyous view of "home" as eternal, with this blessed faith that, though the household here below may have its vacant chambers and its broken hearts, still, above with God, the shattered strings are readjusted and the family harp set to better and loftier music, and to nobler tone, and a perfect and beautiful harmony reached, with such a view. I say, do these earthly dwellings become lighted up with majestic splendor, and the inward altar is continually adorned and strengthened by cherubim and seraphim. Nay, then, when the funeral bell tolls, there is no utter despair, no complete rebellion, no desire to question the doings of God, but the grand conception that the loved are not lost, the dear ones not really vanished, but that the reunion will come and a new mansion be established, where no more partings can possibly take place.

Secondly, we have the fellowship of mental powers in heaven, or mansions of congenial minds. Here is a most important truth. Often here on earth we are thrown in perpetual contact with those who can never appreciate us. There seems to be no point of a true communion. But not so will it be in God's city. There a Plato will find a Plato; Socrates, another one like himself; Fénelon, Fénelon; so on through the eternal range. Even Jesus finds God, of whom he is the perfect image.

How often we each say here, "I am misunderstood"! but that we can never say there.

For every lofty idea, for every brilliant thought, and for every kindling resolve there is a beautiful companionship, so that Milton and Newton and Pascal can take each other by the hand; nay more, so that all struggling students can find an applauding crowd.

I know some say, "Oh, he was a brave scholar here, but that will avail nothing in heaven; and all his brilliant culture is but so much waste power there, for there are no dividends after death for the loftiest brain that ever lived, and ideas are only of the earth, earthy."

I say, no such thing! God forbid! Because mind is not everything, it does not follow that it is nothing. Newton and the idiot do not stand on a level right away on the other side.

Why, how empty all scholarship would be, how hollow all genius, and what a mournful dirge all the gracious scintillations of a great mind, if the expiring breath closed the account, so that the owner never again could claim his own creation!

Then a huge library would be one of the saddest sights in the world; for, as we read off the names of the various authors there revealed, we should be appalled by the thought that the giants were now babes, and their dearest efforts of no avail in the great sweep of eternity. Not so, my brother! Never so, my sister! Everything we know here will have its splendid fruitage in God's city. Knowledge is power forever. The mind never dies. If Newton picked up his pebbles of truth on the shore of infinite truth while he dwelt here, so much the more now, and so much the easier and the better now, from the fact of a former blessed experience, does he pick up larger pebbles — nay, huge diamonds — in the "City of our God."

Nay, more! Not only does he pick these diamonds up, but he has a large circle of friends who know that they are diamonds, and who can, with him, search out the great mysteries of God's glories. I love to think of mental homes, where the great minds frequently gather. Just let us enter one of them by dream. Letting alone the great minds of the Bible, whom else of later days do we find gathered there? Chaucer, Kempis, Hooker, Pascal, Milton, Newton, Addison, Franklin, Everett, Edwards, Ballou, Channing, King, Brooks, Walker, — ay, thousands of others, — each helping the other and all full of the fire of acquisition.

Ah, could we but just hear them speak, how much better would they teach us now! Of course, now they see that a great deal of that which on earth seemed to them true is only partially true, and much that they called grand is to them now but as the rattle of the child to the grown-up man. They see with larger eyes, they hear with finer ears; and all clogs are taken away from their thoughts, so that now, were they to rewrite their works, they would make a great many changes. Yet they thank God, I know, that here they gave their minds full sweep, and tried to the best of their strength to find out the secrets of the world. Is it not, then, a grand idea that we lose nothing by thinking and by studying, and that every investment which we make of the mind's best powers shall yield its glorious dividend in the bank of heaven? But, last and best of all, there are mansions in heaven where the most finished, cultured, and growing souls can have a happy communion.

Soul-mansions we may call them. Goodness takes the lead in heaven. I love to think of homes there, where all the good ones from the days of Genesis till now frequently gather to chant the glory of God and to find some way of enlarging and enriching character. Here, too, I believe these noble spirits converse together as to the best way of helping those less noble.

They form their glorious plans how to train lower spirits, so that those in the primary school of heaven can in time reach the highest class in God's college. Nay, more: I believe they apportion certain numbers to visit earth as guardian angels over poor mortals, that we may be saved from temptation, become penitent for sin, be soothed in sorrow, be prepared to die, and have an easy passage into eternity. I believe, too, that these good ones influence us all the time on our better side, so that many of the noble deeds done upon the earth are but the unconscious echoes of the whispers of angels.

It is not a fancy that every one of us has a special guardian angel around us all the time, night and day, till the last breath be taken.

So, too, up in that great council chamber of the noble angels there are reports given of our character, of our growth and our loss, of our gains and our slips; and new efforts are suggested for our advance or rescue.

You had a wrong thought last week, or you told a falsehood, or you performed a naughty or wicked deed. Well, your guardian angel saw all that you did; and your conduct, not in anger nor even blame, was reported, while the purest spirits in heaven held a council how to save you. And I sometimes think they will not let you alone till they do save you: they will beset you continually till they get you straight on your feet.

Now, when you consider how many people there are in the earth, and when you think that each one is certainly guarded by one angel and many by whole legions of angels, you must be aware that there will be enough to do in the council chambers of the holy all the time for the upbuilding and cleansing of the world. You may call all this fancy. So is everything in the world before it becomes fact. Fancy always precedes fact. So all our greatest discoveries have been reached. Everything is guessed out before it is worked out.

Thus we get the law of gravity, the full power of electricity, the force of steam, the history of the stars, and the curious facts of all science. Thus, without doubt, are we allowed to grasp many of the grandest of God's truths. The Bible is sprinkled full of glorious hints and problems that we must work out. Ah, my friends! we reach reality only through the holy baptism of thought and from a deep and earnest communion of the spirit with the mysterious truths of God.

We want a ladder placed between our hearts and the holy city, that we may constantly climb for clearer proofs of the kind Providence that watches our every breath and step. Let us always be willing to keep open ears and consecrated hearts, that thus our way on earth may be bright, beautiful, sweet, grand, and sacred, and our entrance into the higher life an apocalypse of glory and splendor.

"In my Father's house are many mansions." Yes, my friends; but we shall get into those mansions safely only in one way,— through the aid of the Lord Jesus Christ.

Alice Cary, who a few years ago passed over the river, has beautifully said: —

> " One sweetly solemn thought
>   Comes to me o'er and o'er :
> I am nearer home to-day
>   Than I ever was before.
>
> " Nearer my Father's house,
>   Where the many mansions be,
> Nearer the great white throne,
>   Nearer the jasper sea.

"Nearer the bound of life,
    Where we lay our burdens down,
Nearer leaving the cross,
    Nearer wearing the crown.

"Saviour, perfect my trust,
    Strengthen my might of faith,
Let me feel as I would when I stand
    On the rock of the shore of death.

"Feel as I would when my feet
    Are slipping over the brink;
For it may be I'm nearer home,
    Nearer now than I think."

Yes, my friends, the many mansions where families are gathered, where mental power meets its beautiful fellowship, and where holy souls are blessed with a joyous companionship, can only be reached with full peace when Jesus is at our side and holds our hand. May he, our Redeemer and our Lord, have mercy upon us! May he, in God's good time, lead us safely into everlasting joy!

Now, in those mansions who are waiting for us?

What dear ones are lonely without us whose departure almost made our hearts marble and sent a deep cloud over all our future? Is it the little child, whose beaming face, joyous laugh, confidential talk, and constant companionship made every day celestial and all our thoughts glad? Well, that child is still bright and beautiful, and watches us yet with tender and holy interest, and is waiting to clasp us once more in a greeting that shall be eternal.

Is it the grown-up son and daughter that have gone into the eternal home just when most needed here, just when panoplied for a grand earthly success, and just as we were rejoicing with a holy and just pride for the great gift God so graciously put into our hands? Well, those lost ones are all safe, and still full of hope, joy, and faith, and still worthy of our congratulation and fellowship. They also stand by our side with watchful eyes and constant gifts, shielding and helping and blessing us continually.

Is it old age that has gone from us, old in goodness, rich in holy fruit, and mellowed and hallowed by a long practice of beneficence and love,— a father or mother, honored, trusted, and served, ay, almost worshipped? Well, it is all right. The dear ones are not gone, they are not lost, they are not a great way off; and they still befriend, sanctify, and besiege our steps with choice benedictions and with gracious smiles.

Yes, my friends, all those that we have seemingly lost are keeping house on the other side of the river; and they will be waiting at the door when we, too, are called, and, oh, such a greeting!

Ah, the bliss, the joy, and the glory of that sacred and touching hour, as we take each other again by the hand and look each other again in the eye, and meet never more to part!

IV.

MORDECAI SITTING AT THE KING'S GATE.

"All this availeth me nothing so long as I see Mordecai, the Jew, sitting at the king's gate."—ESTHER v. 13.

KING AHASUERUS had raised Haman to a position of great eminence, mighty power, and splendid renown, where he could secure large wealth, an extensive influence, and be honored abundantly in the nation where he dwelt; and Esther, the wife of the king, had invited Haman to a feast which she had prepared for her husband and his distinguished minister. Yet, while encircled by all these advantages, at the very flush of his great success, as he was the first man in the kingdom and was living like a prince, Haman was dissatisfied, a cloud was upon his brow, and a canker rested upon his heart. So he returned to his home. Then he sent and called for his friends and Zerish, his wife, and told them of the glory of his riches, the multitude of his children, all the things wherein the king had promoted him, how he had advanced him above the princes and servants of the king, how Esther, the queen, did let no man come in with the king unto the banquet which she had prepared but himself, and that on the morrow he was again invited to the banquet; yet Haman said, "All this availeth me nothing so long as I see Mordecai, the Jew, sitting at the king's gate."

Now, this Mordecai, the Jew, was the only man who refused to do honor to the wicked Haman; for he had read his character thoroughly, notwithstanding the coat of varnish that somewhat concealed it, and so he had too much self-respect to do homage to one who so little deserved it. And simply because this one man of a nation despised, who was a foreigner and who was living in the kingdom only by permit,— simply because this stranger at the gate would not notice the prime minister, all the rest of the great man's privileges, glories, and honors crumble to dust, while all his life becomes sadly embittered, poisoned, and shattered! The whole scene is so richly descriptive of every-day life, so clearly, so forcibly, and so earnestly reveals a vein in everybody's nature, and there are so many Hamans and Mordecais living to-day, that I have felt it a duty, as well as a pleasure and a privilege, as well as an inclination, to derive from the account some lesson that shall lead us to a deeper, a holier, and a more genial consecration of our whole hearts to goodness, to honor, and to truth. Every one of us would be perfectly happy, were it not for the lamentable fact that some "Mordecai" sits at our gate.

We have all that we need, are covered, crowned, and overwhelmed with bounties, and God has been exceedingly liberal with us, and the sunshine of his favor is ever constant, bright, and beautiful, and all these things we are ready to allow; but, oh, that everlasting, that ever-shameful, and that always terrible "but"! There is some mole-hill in our way, some little defect, a small spot of dust, that to our distorted vision looks just like a mountain; and so our whole life is thereby shadowed, outraged, and distorted, and over all our hopes, favors, and deeds a fearful gloom is spread. Something is in our way. Perhaps no real thing, — only a phantasy raised in the brain, only a poisoned vapor exhaled by the bewitched imagination, a creation of nervousness, a product of fear, the spasm of a dream, a mote in the air, something impalpable, thin, and made up of foam; but, oh, how real it seems to us, how threatening, how impenetrable, how like a great rock or a huge mountain! It is our Mordecai, sitting at the gate, making faces at us, insulting us, and aiming at us deadly weapons for our sure destruction; and, brothers and sisters, if we will only use our judgment, reason, tact, and common sense, such obstructions will vanish, the enemy will be gone, and our foolish visions will dissolve into nothingness. It has been said by those well versed in the history of the human race that it would be an impossible thing to discover a perfectly contented person; that is, to find anybody who had all that was wanted, who desired nothing more, who was wholly free from envy, jealousy, ambition, and who cast no longing eyes on the possessions, gifts, and advantages of anybody else.

We are always wanting a little more than what God has given to us, while the more we receive the still more craving do we become, and there is no limit to our demands; while the slightest difficulty obstructing us in our reachings after greater gains, although the trouble be as fine as the point of a needle, vitiates, poisons, and shuts out our gratitude for what we have already received, and converts us into miserable misanthropes, fills us with a wretched peevishness, corrupts our whole existence, changes us into very unhappy specimens of humanity, and God *must* continually give to us, or by some strange fatality we always think that we have a right to complain. It is a curious fact in human nature that a great many people seldom, if ever, attempt to count their blessings, but are constantly looking the other way, and are ever brooding over real or supposed deprivations, and are gazing at the spectres in the air. Should a man for seventy years be especially favored by Providence with health, fortune, and friends, and then at once lose, or seem to be in danger of losing, one or all, the years of providential watching, bounty, and benediction would gradually fade out of sight, escape out of memory, and float into thin vapor, while present misery or the fear of it would suffocate the affections and erase all piety from the soul.

When everything goes well with us, and when our whole life is one constant victory, we are apt to concentrate our thoughts upon ourselves, so that we forget heaven, earth, and everything except our own glory and power. But let a reverse come, then we exclaim, quite readily, Why has God so dealt with us?

I have always been convinced that God does more for us than against us; and I know that, if we looked only on the bright side of life, and traced the golden streaks that permeate, invest, and glorify life with the splendors that arch it so wonderfully, we should find all our trials melting away, or taking a new, brilliant, and gracious color, and putting on a fresh, an attractive, and spiritual nature. But no: this is not the way with a great many. They prefer to live in a storm, and look all the time purposely, petulantly, and sadly to where "Mordecai sits at the gate." Now where is our Mordecai? Gaze at a few imaginary cases. One has wealth, to all appearances,— abundance of it. It keeps increasing year by year, and vast are the comforts which it secures for its possessor. And yet this one is not happy; for he sees with his troubled eyes somebody more honored, perhaps not commanding the use of so much coin, but gaining more credit, respect, and authority, and then all his pleasure departs, his gold becomes dross, and he lives poverty-stricken in the centre of his splendors, opulent in everything save in that which of all things is most desirable,— save in character, reputation, and the sweet peace of the heart. One has great learning, understands many languages, is full of book knowledge, and is a perfect encyclopædia of facts, and yet, notwithstanding these immense advantages, lacks, perhaps, practical force, and is disheartened, mortified, and overwhelmed by seeing another man, not half so learned, wielding a larger literary power, securing a wider influence, and taking captive the ears and the hearts of the public.

Again, some one has striven hard to be a Christian, to become devout in faith, liberal in practice, charitable to all men, and yet is cast down, saddened, and made morose at seeing another whose principles are false, whose heart is hollow, but whose hypocrisy is deep, gaining great reputation for sanctity, standing higher than himself (who is really the earnest, persistent, and holy disciple), attracting more attention in the opinions of Christians, and gazed upon, until the fall comes, as one of the bulwarks of the Church. So the man of wealth, the man of letters, and the man of piety all have their Mordecais; while their coin, literature, and religion are somewhat corrupted, and their whole characters considerably tinged and darkened thereby.

Friends, am I sketching pictures of fancy merely? Have I gone, in my illustrations, beyond the regions of common experience and common sense? And have I been dwelling in dreamland, and outside entirely of anything that relates to daily events and to each one's human nature? Let us ask our own hearts. Let us sift our own biographies, and let a week's living speak for us; and then I am willing to abide the reply! Now, how are we to get rid of our Mordecais? If they are with us, if they sit at our gate, and if they continually excite our pride, anger, and ambition, why the sooner they are put out of our way and out of our thoughts the better; for of no use would a gaze at the difficulty become unless we were to plan some way of rooting it out and of consigning it to oblivion.

We are not to follow Haman's plan of cure, and we must not copy his high-handed measures, else perchance we may perish, like him, on the same scaffold which we prepare for our enemies; for every ill thing which we prepare for the injury of another is very apt, sooner or later, to rebound against ourselves. It will do us no good, and it will do our seeming opponents no harm, to rail at them, and to attempt to injure them in any way; and, in fact, our ill speech and ill usage will only confirm them in their opposition, increase our own bad temper, heighten the difficulty instead of removing it, and throw us into a deeper distress. But, friends, instead of abusing, let us treat with a distinguished courtesy, a hearty kindness, and a holy benevolence all those who seem to stand in our way; for nothing will so soon drive away the mirage that obscures our vision as this gentle method of dealing with our rivals.

Had Haman endeavored to obtain Mordecai's friendship, engirdled him with favors, disregarded entirely his lack of courtesy, and always addressed him tenderly, sought his advice, and encouraged him in all ways, he would have completely conquered his enmity, he would have stolen all the iron from his heart, and he would have secured the good will of Esther and Ahasuerus, have built up securely his own prosperity, and have found in the Jew an ardent admirer and a confidential friend.

We can only get rid of our difficulties by changing them into helps, we can only conquer our opposers by making them friends; and there is a great deal of good common sense in the command of the apostle Paul when he says that we must heap coals of fire upon the heads of our enemies; for he means, as we see by the chapter, the fire of kindness, for nothing will so quickly thaw an icy hatred as a hearty, holy, and blessed love. We may always be sure that we shall baffle our opponents when we prove to them that, do what they will for our harm and plan what they can for our injury, that we still look upon them as friends, shall still treat them, as far as we are able, with a hearty, a holy, and a splendid good will; and seeming, or real, enemies, thus treated, are attacked on the very side not fortified for defence, are forced to surrender against such an unexpected contagious and blazing fire, their hearts are torn right open, and they cannot be Mordecais any longer, while their whole natures become sweetened, and they at once enlist on our side, become our royal defenders, thorough champions, and everlasting friends. But, supposing we had no human way of getting rid of our difficulties, that we had tried everything, while everything had failed; suppose, in spite of all we can do, think, and say, the Jew will continue to sit at the gate, and mock, irritate, and abuse us in all ways, upsetting all our plans, throwing us into great confusion, and putting thorns in the flesh forever,— is there, then, no help, light, peace, and joy? Are we ever to be in the dark, are we to call life a failure, and are we to label opportunity only as a delusion? Ah, no! we still have an escape, help, and light, if we will follow strictly the spirit of Christ's commands; for Jesus tells us not to lean on arms of flesh, and not to trust to man, to look only to God and himself, and keep our eyes so upward fixed as to care for no earthly trial and be ruffled by no worldly disappointment. Mordecai sits at the gate! Well, let him sit there forever; and we will not look at him nor think of him nor care about him, for we have better work to do than to be troubled about his concerns. Our duty calls us another way, and we care for no approbation nor disapprobation save that which comes from Almighty God.

If we keep in this Christ-like spirit, we shall always conquer our troubles, disarm our opponents, and easily dismantle their cannon, demolish their forts, and cause them to beat a disastrous retreat. If we will only aim highly enough, all the teasing annoyances of life will quickly fade away; and, if we will only "look aloft," our brows will never be discomposed, our whole existence will be serene, and we shall at last sweetly sink to sleep, leaving behind us, as a precious legacy, an aroma of goodness that will charm many a soul into loyal discipleship and lead whole crowds into the ranks of the Good Shepherd and Bishop of souls. And God grant that we may thus dispose of all things that trouble us, and charm all our difficulties into vacuity. "All this availeth me nothing, so long as I see Mordecai, the Jew, sitting at the king's gate."

Availeth us nothing, do we say? Then it is our own fault, our own disgrace; and we ought to be ashamed to make the confession, and still more ashamed to cherish such a troubled, sharp, and acid disposition. This is what I would say to all the Hamans all over the earth, that they are bidden by God, Jesus, all good angels, by the claims of honor, truth, and purity, because they have souls and are immortal,— they are bidden, and seriously urged, to make their seeming disadvantages and all their discipline avail them something, to make them the bulwark of their safety, the chart of their saintship, and the very buttress and true foundation of their spiritual life. Let us all throw aside envy, despair, a false ambition, and then let us strive to obtain an unsullied greatness, a spotless goodness, and a real good-nature through a glorious, a sublime, and an everlasting fellowship with the Lord Jesus Christ. So may it be, Almighty God!

V.

NEW THINGS.

"Some new thing."— ACTS xvii. 21.

LET it be clearly understood that in what I have to say I do not intend to impeach the old or the new, but I wish to bring the best part of both into a holy reconciliation. Some new thing! That was the great trouble with the Athenians,— the looking for new things. It is a disease that is common to us all, and it is an affliction which will be very likely to continue for a great while. For some people make it their creed that anything old is bad, and that anything fresh, just because it is fresh, must be right, true, and grand; and such persons change with every drifting tide of circumstance, and are whirled along by the gales of events, so that you never know where to find them, for you look and they are there, and you look again and they are gone, and what they are to-day is by no means a test of what they will be to-morrow, and the next year they will deny all they have said and advocated the three hundred and sixty-five days before. And they call their advance progress; and, if progress means motion, commotion, revolution, and a whirlwind, they are right! Now I wish to set forth that the peace of society is disturbed by such innovators; and I would maintain that they do as much harm — nay, more harm — than the old settlers, however much mistaken they may be, who never want to change their base, who are satisfied with things as they are, and who are afraid of anything new. The great question with the human heart should be, not always a new thing, not always an old thing, but forever the right thing, be it new or be it old, and no matter whether it have the white locks of the patriarch or the few scattering hairs of the infant. Of course, no great raging desire is planted in the human bosom that does not betoken some grand reality as its pith, prophecy, and intended result, so that the longing for novelty really has its better side, its inspiriting hintings, its grand echoes, and is not all the mark of a restless folly, the foam of an empty spirit, and the sign of a revolutionary soul.

The triumphs of religion, the arts, the sciences, and of everything good, spring from this embryonic principle of uneasiness; and civilization is a continued revelation obtained by the striving for something more and something fresh, or by the dressing up of the old with another garment. Many think that the world is ever repeating itself, so that everything which is has been, seemingly discovered by us, but many times discovered before; but, however this may be, one thing is certain, — that every age must have its dissatisfactions, must try to find, must inquire for, and must search after a new thing. I cannot say, and no one can say, that the power of steam, ether, and electricity is something that our own age has developed; but this we can say, that the proclamation of that power came in this age, because the need was felt just in our day.

So of religion: people may talk as eloquently as they please of one unchangeable religion all the way along from Christ till now, or all the way along from Adam till now, if you will,— and, thanks be to God, it is the one unalterable truth!— but the way of conveying its simplest facts to the minds of the people must vary with each age, or else religion on the human side will ever be in its infancy, and the dissatisfaction arising in many souls against any form of religion as yet presented, provided the objectors do not wish to touch any of the cardinal points of faith, but only rebel against the robes that such points have worn, and simply offer what seems to be a more becoming dress, does not invalidate in the least the claims of the restless ones to a Christian fellowship, courtesy, and name. For only by just such reclothing, during the centuries that have passed, has Christianity obtained its beautiful, sacred, and majestic hold of the hearts of the race.

I have spoken of the yearning for added revelations, so widely prevalent, on its better side, simply to assure you that, while I intend mainly to arraign the innovating spirit as an offence, I have not been unaware of the pleas that such spirit would offer in its defence, nor forgetful that it had a better side, nor disposed to deny that all gains are based on constant changes. Now let me say that this perpetual longing for something new, intellectually, legally, morally, and theologically, tends to create a vast amount of confusion, and leads frequently to a terrible amount of evil; and I believe in holding on to what we have, until we can clearly see our way to something better. Intellectually, we get in the dark by craving variety rather than reality, by loving a smart idea rather than a sound thought, by catering to brilliancy rather than bowing before power, by preferring the fireworks of the imagination to the cannon-balls of the judgment. Take that simplest fact of the books that are used by our children at school, and do we not sometimes think that change is not always improvement? Any one who has been a member of the "Board of School Committee," or connected at any time with a publishing house, or who has been a teacher in any of our public schools, will readily see that during the last fifty years, while there have been myriad of changes in the way of instruction and in the volumes that are used, yet no one under the new plan has exceeded in mental power Edward Everett or Daniel Webster or Rufus Choate. Said a cultivated teacher to me, "The books that are constantly being introduced into our schools are sometimes so very peculiar that I have to study them all out at home before I dare to use them with the class, and I have never yet seen any real advantage in so many troublesome changes."

But not in school alone, but all through life, the presentation of ideas, under fresh formulas, has as often mystified as enlightened the race; and all the books issued are by no means an advance on the old methods of proclamation. Nay: they often obscure what they would illustrate, and throw over what would otherwise have been plain a massive cloud; and the promised better frequently turns out to be a solid worse.

How many lives of Christ have been written! some of them, too, very good; but have they any of them added very greatly to the beauty, strength, and glory of the simple evangelical account? And, since Galileo, Copernicus, Newton, and Kepler, how many philosophers and philosophies have arisen! and yet have we met with any very decided gains?

Legally, too, what is called progress is often only a loss, a blur, and a mistake; and there really has not been much acquired in this way since the Roman laws were made so compact, strong, and grand, or, perhaps, the cardinal points of law have not been strengthened since the great lawgiver, Moses, established the principles of justice, unless we exclude in this judgment the softer tints, the sweeter fragrance, and the more glorious echoes of the "Sermon on the Mount." All the lawgivers in the world may meet and legislatures may legislate till eternity ends, and the grand fundamentals of right will remain the same; and all the oratory in the world cannot swing them from their base with any advantage to the children of God. Murder has been murder ever since Cain killed Abel, and so with all the other vices;

and no new rhetoric or logic can alter the stern and tremendous fact, for justice came to earth full clad from the very beginning of the ages, and nothing could be added to it since then to enhance its dignity, increase its glory, and make it any the more prominent and potent in the regulation of the affairs of men. Nor can any code of morals be brought forward as having any superiority to that which we find established and set forth in the Bible, but most especially and clearly in the New Testament; for duty has the advantage of being old.

While, of course, there may be ever-changing applications of principles, the principles are the same forever. The "Sermon on the Mount" cannot be improved; and it only remains for us to carry out its spirit more and more, and to develop, with all possible power, its hidden beauty, sacred unction, and holy splendor. When any one looks me in the face and tells me that somebody to-day can teach just as well, or better, than Jesus Christ, my Lord and my Redeemer, I feel that such a person is laboring under a great, terrible, and fatal mistake. You may tell me that it is only a theory with such a speaker, and as such betokens nothing and can do no possible harm; but I tell you such a theory, that strives to emasculate the New Testament, that makes Jesus only one among many other teachers, and not a perfect character that can never be copied, and that calls the precepts of our Lord good for that time, but not good for all time, promising something better for a refreshment to-day, — such a theory will not stay in the regions of the brain, and will not wreathe itself merely upon the fancy, but will drop, in a great many cases, its gall upon the heart, scatter its poison into the hand, and make us all unsafe and unhappy.

So every day do we hear scholars talking about a new theology; and we have been promised a new theology ever since Christ left the earth, while the Church, on the human side of it, has been splintered into fragments by the vague promises, empty performances, and futile gifts of those who want to give us something better than the good old Bible. The very attempt in the early Christian centuries to improve the simplicity of the gospel by binding it to strict formulas of man-made definitions was a blow at the grandeur of the great Book that has recoiled against the authors ever since; for God's Book, in every necessary part, was plain enough without any mortal dictionary, and the very moment that definition came obscurity commenced. They were called "Christians" first at Antioch; and what a pity that any other name was ever invented! for, in striving after greater things, the Church fell into the mire at once, and it will stay in the mire till we go back to Antioch, and take our Bible and our Master, and nothing more and nothing less, for our guide, motto, and inspiration, and then will the world soon be swept clean of all sin, idolatry, and confusion.

Gracious Father, a new theology! and how can this thing be? A new *Theoû Logos*, a fresh definition of

God? Why, who shall write it, who shall think it, and who shall dare make it known? For it must be some one better than Christ and better than God, for the old discourse about God came through the Father by the Son, and was ratified as a complete revelation at the time of its grand, majestic, and sacred disclosure; and who, then, shall this wonderful teacher be? I say, let us go back instead of going forward here.

Let us go back to Nazareth, Jerusalem, Bethlehem, to all Judea, and to all Syria, let us go back to the first Christian church, at its early start, and we shall learn all that is necessary about the great Ruler of the heavens and the earth, while much that obscures our faith at the present hour will be entirely thrown into oblivion. I stand up to-day, then, to plead for all old things that are good, while I protest most heartily against that rash spirit of the age that would cut itself entirely off from the past, and rush headlong into the future; and I am always afraid of progress when it throws off the balance-wheel of experience. Nay: advance, that strives to cauterize what has been, destroys itself; and it would be as if the roof of a house should order every story below it to be demolished, which is simply, indirectly, and only asking for its own grave at the same time. I believe in growth; but it must be like that which is seen when the youth issues from the babe, and like that which is developed when the man springs from the youth,— that is, it must be step by step, while identity is constantly preserved and the forward must ever be linked to the backward by precious memories, sacred discipline, and the fragrance of noble victories.

There are divine laws that regulate events, gains, revelations, and new things as well, as closely, and as sacredly as they do all life, so that development outside of Heaven's law will simply be another name for shame, destruction, and death; and the laws of a true growth can be easily ascertained by the thoughtful mind, religious heart, and loving soul if a few hundred years be faithfully scanned, for then it will be seen that the movements of Providence are slow, steady, and sure, and are links in a chain reaching way backward to creation and way forward into eternity. Some new thing! Well, if it be true, as some say, that there is no new thing under the sun, but that all things which we call so are but photographs of some forgotten discoveries that are buried in the dim ages of the past, there is yet a way of looking at the matter by which we may most certainly be encouraged; namely, there are new methods of describing what we suppose we invent, fresh illustrations, kindling descriptions, racy, burning, and uplifting rhetoric, such as no ages of the past could possibly reveal, and, then again, there is a moral and a spiritual view of looking at the world and at God's dealings with his children that will give the most glorious, comforting, and blessed definitions to everything that occurs, by which we not only obtain "new things," but a new way of looking at everything, and there is what we may call an optimism as well as a pessimism in the definition of events. Here are a few paragraphs that fell into my hands the other day, and they gave me great pleasure: —

"Two boys went to hunt for grapes; and one was happy because he found them, and the other was angry because he found seeds in them."

"Two men recovered from sickness. One said, 'I am better to-day': the other said, 'I was worse yesterday.'"

"Two persons gazed at a bush. One said, 'It has a rose': the other said, 'It has a thorn.'"

"'I am glad that I live,' said one man: 'I am sorry that I must die,' said his brother."

"Two persons had bees. One called them 'honey-bees': the other said they were 'stinging bees.'"

So it is ever, my friends; for we discover pretty much what we like, or what by our carefulness we strive to obtain, or what by the grace of Almighty God our eyes are open to see.

We want some new thing. Well, the more we become acquainted with the Christ, who is the same yesterday, to-day, and forever, and the more we obey his glorious precepts, the more clearly, fully, and gloriously shall we receive what we want; for that character has ever something beautiful to reveal to the earnest seeker, and the precepts of the Lord are so full of wisdom, righteousness, and glory that it will take more than eternity to exhaust their splendid power, beautiful promise, and holy consolation. Let us cling, then, to Jesus Christ, so that everything shall be bright, sweet, sacred, fresh, glorious, and triumphant, and so that, as we enter the kingdom above, each one of us shall hear those uplifting words: "Well done, good and faithful servant! Enter thou into the joy of thy Lord!"

VI.

CAN GOD BE DISCOVERED?

"Canst thou by searching find out God?" — JOB xi. 7.

YES, to a certain extent, we can find out God. That is to say, we are not able to measure the whole of the Infinite, since that would be impossible, even on the ground of philosophy alone; for how can finite grasp Infinite? Yet God we can apprehend, find out, realize, and appropriate, if we may reverently say so, by degrees, little by little, as our souls grow toward heaven, and as our hearts become spiritualized; for it is promised "that the pure in heart shall see God."

But perhaps even here we should make a qualification that what we want to say this morning may be clearly understood; namely, the nature of God is a mystery, and no human plummet, however deep or rich or strong or beautiful or grand or mighty, can unravel that. But the character of the dear Father of us all grows more plain, more clear, more grand, and more sublime as we grow more holy; and it is revealed in ever renewed and increased glory, giving us fresh splendors, like the revolving kaleidoscope, every time that we cause our sanctified will to move in the right line. What, then, are the laws of our access to God, keeping always in mind, of course, that our own spiritual life is the mightiest lever for lifting us into this great light? The Father is revealed in nature and in revelation and in our own souls; and the best men and the best women in the world are the ones who can see this fact the clearest and the most gratefully acknowledge it with a true joy and a sacred love.

For a long while in the history of the world it was only in nature that the gods were found; and then puzzled minds, forgetting that Infinite Power needed only a unit for its expression, thought that a Deity must be created for every special need. Still, the expression of worship, even under this sad mistake, was a mark of devotion and trust for which every soul to-day ought to be glad.

"Canst thou by searching find out God?" Why, yes, ever since man was made in the very twilight of the ages, ere the auroral light hardly tinged the sky of time, we find the mortal looking after the Eternal Father in sun, moon, and stars, in forests and waters, in everything and all things that human ken could not grasp nor earthly strength manage. Certainly, all the good that ever came to the ancients reached them in this way. In spite of idolatry and sin, letting alone base superstition and idle fancy and everything strange and sad, yet here, in the upturned eye and in the outstretched hand and in the prostrate body, I cannot help seeing and admiring the presence and the spirit and the might of worship, the infant's prattle concerning eternal realities; and sometimes, too, we hear exclamations that startle us by their grandeur, and are full of promise and peace. Listen to a few of these breathings toward heaven. Some one says, thousands of years ago: "In the beginning there arose the Source of golden light. He was the only born Lord of all that is. He established the earth and the sky. Who is the God to whom we shall offer our sacrifice? He who gives life, he who gives strength, whose blessing all the bright gods desire, whose shadow is immortality, whose shadow is death."

Yet more: "I see Thy glory still like sunset on a mountain's head. . . . God, all knowing, deliver from the crooked path of sin! From the unreal lead me to the real, from darkness to light, from death to immortality." And again: "There is no end to misery save in the knowledge of God. . . . The Creator, the Being without fear, without enmity, Everlasting One, the Self-existing. . . . O God, under thy power all has been done: naught is of myself." Such, my friends, are the words of those who had nature alone for their teacher; and what do you think of such grand inspirations? Would you treat harshly those that have such liftings up of the spirit? Would you not say that a great deal of heaven's truth is let down into all minds? But, if once the voice was so great, so tender, and so sublime to those apparently so benighted, how now to-day, this hour, with us, with all the privileges that nineteen centuries have poured upon us, with such majestic beauty and with such splendid profusion? Can we not find out a great deal up above, all around, down beneath, and everywhere from this grand cathedral of space in which God has placed us, even supposing for a moment there were no Bibles, and nothing whatever but what the outward sight reveals?

Do you tell me that science votes the other way, and that, the wiser we grow, the thicker are our denials and the deeper distrust we have of everything save our own keen wit? Do you point me to a number of astronomers and anatomists and geologists who are arrant sceptics and seeming atheists, and then smilingly assume that we had better keep in the dark unless we want to be all dark forever? I tell you, Nay. I am sure that all such statements that are derogatory to knowledge are a mournful impeachment against the Eternal Mind, by whom all things are governed and sustained. So, too, would I confidently assert that the majority of our strong men in "natural philosophy" are men of large faith, who seem to have all heaven beating on their hearts. I care not what two eminent scholars said a few years ago (and their words found a passage through the cable with a wonderful and a mournful echo), yet I still affirm that the weight of intellect is on the believing side; and why not? By what quicker road can I travel to God and to a good God than by astronomy, that, throughout all its minutest items, bathes me in such splendors that must inevitably lead me at once to adore the Author and Maker of us all?

If I am whirling around the sun with a fearful rapidity, who keeps me from being dizzy, and who saves me from falling, and who holds me safe from death? If the sun carries such intense heat, what saves the world from being destroyed by fire? What holds the stars up that they do not fall, and who causes the moon to act as servant to the sun, so that the darkness of the night shall not reign supreme?

What keeps the constantly recurring comets from touching the earth, and thus closing the account with all of us? When the rain falls, why not a perpetual flood? And, as the snowflakes come, why are we not buried out of sight by the whirling drifts? You may tell me of laws; but I reply, Laws are dumb. Then I ask you, Who made the laws of which you speak? You have discovered them, or twinkles of them, perhaps; but you did not make them, and they were not self-created, and I confidently appeal unto the Maker of them all. Like Saint Paul of old, I appeal to the great King of kings. So, too, look at your body. How did all these bones leap into substance and slide into place and borrow flesh for a garment? Also, when these bodies of ours were formed, how came we to have a brain and a soul? Do you answer, Mere chance? Nothing but madness can say that; for how is it that chance has once done that which it has never been able to copy in anything else, or to surpass at any time? And how is it that accident is so often repeated in just the same shape age after age? The study of ourselves inevitably, irresistibly, and immediately leads us up to the great King of kings.

Again, take geology through all its secret grandeur and all its massive revelations, way back in the beginning and way up to the present hour, and you must in every rock and in every stone and in every clod of earth, way down in the deep crust and way through all the stratas, in each age as it appears, and in all the relics that are upheaved,— you must, I say, find an organizing mind more than mortal's, that is eternal in the heavens. Do you tell me, again, that rock can create rock, that mere material substance can produce a succession forever and ever, and that thus materialism is the secret of all growth, splendor, and beauty? Well, then, you simply give a different name to God, but a name that is an absurdity, unless a Divine Being is behind and in and through it all. Once more, do you tell me that I must let science alone if I want to be soundly, devoutly, truly religious, and a real child of God? Is it possible that you mean what you say?

Here are the footprints of the great Architect; and must I wash those footprints out, as of no meaning and as of dangerous tendency, and as not girdled with any spiritual power? Again I tell you nay. God has written me a letter, in all the splendors of this earth and of the heavens; and I must and I will read it, wherever I please, and, as I read it, every line speaks of him, of his might, of his beauty, of his grandeur, of his protecting care, of his overwhelming goodness, and of his all-pervading presence. But, thanks be to his holy name, he has not only written me a letter, but he has sent me a Messenger, fearing I might not perhaps read all of this letter aright; and this is my second point,— that we find him, the Father, through revelation, as of course it appears after Christ has been to this world, and after he, the blessed Lord, has given us the key to all needed mysteries. "Canst thou by searching find out God?" Yes, Job: from Genesis to Apocalypse, if I search for God with a reverent mind and with a teachable spirit, guided all the time by the inspiration of the Holy Ghost, I shall find out a great deal about him; and so would you, if you only had stood when your words were spoken just where I stand to-day.

I find that he is the Creator of the world. I find that he preserves all things by his ever-blessed help. I find that nothing leaps really outside of his eternal Will. I find, too, that none of us can slip away from his care and his yearning throughout everlasting ages; for he has promised, "I will never leave thee nor forsake thee." I find, too,— for he has proclaimed it through his Son,— that he is my Father and my best Friend, and that his goodness and his kindness are beyond all possible measurement. O Job, again I speak to thee, Have I not discovered a good deal? Can earth be lonely now? Can the other life be a dread mystery? Is not the destiny of us all something sublime? and, under these great definitions, does not duty become resplendent and opportunity transcendently glorious?

My hearers, not only do I believe in science, but I believe in the Bible and in the important truths that it contains; and I believe that there is enough in that great Book that all of us can understand, that, rightly received into heart and practice, will make each life full of harmony, beauty, and strength. Let each one of us take what is plain and touching and beyond any shadow of a question, and have just that select portion for continued help and comfort, and a wonderful enlightenment will fall upon every heart, and the very gates of heaven will be opened, and angels will descend and ascend up and down between earth and heaven.

Again, inwardly, in each one's soul, God resides; and he can be found there if we will only search diligently. I admit that he has a very small place sometimes (the head of a needle might perhaps be a generous description of the space that some people give to him); but all entertain him somehow, and even those who deny the fact altogether are yet unwittingly making him a guest. He will not let us alone. He is there now, my brother and my sister, in a large or in a small chamber, right in the centre of your inward life. He wants more room given to him by all of us, and he desires that all of us should search for him the more, that we may continually feel his presence, own his power, and be uplifted by his gracious benediction. Most certainly, too, shall he be found at some moment, even by those who the most stoutly deny his presence. Job says, Find out God;

but perhaps he would have done better, had he said that, by our searching, God in time would be willing to find us out, and would be very glad to own us as his beloved children.

How many things you and I possess that we do not really love and value; but when, through some striking experience, something that was unconsciously ours has become in a special way important to us, how we prize the gift as never before! So, in a higher way, does Almighty God prize us, when we begin to prize him. Always, of course, we belonged to him; but, when we own the relationship and when we rejoice in the privilege and when we are earnest, believing, and loving children, what added joy must spring into that all-gracious Heart! So, as we find God and as God finds us, do we gain all our victories, reach all our gifts, attain all our powers, and become heroes and heroines in the great domain of nature and of spirit. We may think, in the full flush of worldly triumph, that we have lighted our own fires, that we have found our own fuel, and that we have worthily earned the blaze and the heat that are so comfortable and so grand; but we are mistaken, for only as we are in God and as God is in us do we reach unto anything great and majestic and worth the keeping, and there is no victory save the victory that is regulated and secured by Eternal Providence.

Even the great Roman orator, who stood outside of Christ, thus eloquently spoke: "We may admire ourselves, conscript fathers, as much as we please: still, neither by numbers did we vanquish the Spaniards, nor by bodily strength the Gauls, nor by cunning the Carthaginians, nor through the arts the Greeks, but through our devotion and our religious feeling."

Can we by searching find out God? I think that Jesus says, expressly, Yes. For he says, "He that hath seen me hath seen the Father"; and he also says "that those who go to him he will in no wise cast out." Perhaps we could throw the whole argument and spirit of what we have attempted to say, with the noble plea and call of the Lord, in some such lines as these that I have taken the liberty to throw together in a poetic form: —

> Go, then, to Christ, and ask of him
>   The way to God and right,
> And all the mighty secrets win
>   Of truths so pure and bright.
>
> Go, then, to Christ, and he will say
>   Why Nature is so grand,
> So filled with God, the light, the way
>   That seeking souls demand.
>
> Go, then, to Christ, and see how clear,
>   By revelation's light,
> Our God is seen! how very near
>   To each and every sight!
>
> Go, then, to Christ; for he will show
>   The voice within is found,
> That all the sons of God may know
>   What place is holy ground.
>
> Thus search out God, and find your peace,
>   And grow in grace and love,
> And give your faith a large increase,
>   Till all shall meet above.

VII.

THE FATAL SUBSTITUTE.

"Send, I pray thee, by the hand of him whom thou wilt send."—
Ex. iv. 13.

THESE words are idiomatic, but in our own language would probably read thus: Send anybody, send everybody; but do not send me. Send somebody else, get a substitute: let me be excused.

And the words were evidently a giving up of the trust, a declination of the honor, and a setting aside, for a moment, of the grand opportunity; for we read in the next verse that the Lord was displeased at the reply of Moses, and would not excuse him from his task, but set him at work at once, with Aaron to help him.

"Send somebody else." So Moses really said. So we are all of us apt to say; and it is this bad habit of putting off on to other people what we ought to do ourselves that I wish to speak about at this time.

I always liked the saying of a former President of the United States, when he thought that it would be best for him to take a position that was opposed by many of the wise men of his day, as he exclaimed, "I will take the responsibility." Not that I approve of all that he said or of all that he did or of all that he was, although I cannot help feeling that he was a very remarkable man; but I do admire his spirit of independence, his readiness to carry out his own idea, and his willingness to do what he thought was right, and I am rejoiced that he did not say, Let somebody else do it: let another person take the responsibility, and, in case of failure, give me a chance to creep away from blame. Send somebody else. No: he took up his own duties in his own name, just as he could measure them, and was willing to stand up squarely to what he thought was right.

Ah! how often we each one of us say, Send somebody else to do my thinking, or to plan my life, or to direct my habits, or to order all my ways, or to do the main part of my work, for we are afraid to take the responsibility; and so we float idly on the stream of time, reduce our lives to zero, and die, leaving no more marks upon the earth than those which are caused by the floating away of the foam on the ocean wave.

How few people dare to think! With a combination lock on the door of the brain, with a knowledge of all the numbers that must be used in the opening of that singular lock, fully acquainted with the turns of the dial ere any progress can be made, familiar with all the movements that will lead to the sliding back of all obstructions, they give the lesson to somebody else, they hand over the key to a substitute, they let another person open the mental safe, and they let that other person deposit there just what he or she may please; and then they look at the property, and arrogantly claim it as their own. Well, how much is their own? The ownership of the safe, the understanding of the mysteries that lead to its use, and the keeping of the key; but, after that, they have recklessly given up their privileges to somebody else.

Oh, what a change would come upon the world, what a glory would descend from the heavens, what opportunities, what splendors, what grand, holy, magnificent, and overwhelming revelations, if every child of God took the full charge of self, managed the thoughts, entered alone, or with Heaven grandly helping, into all the chambers of ideas, and then came before the world fresh, original, strong, sparkling, with glorious thoughts, that are all lighted up by scintillations from God's altar! and, just as we find on the earth copper mines, lead mines, gold mines, silver mines, and iron mines, all different, all valuable, all eagerly developed, and neither one sliding into the other, but all recognizing the value of each, so in the soil of the mind should we find, under a right, righteous, holy, and special culture, all the metals of intellect, bringing us rich treasures, helping all the people, and building up the kingdom of God in all the waste places of the earth. And then the gold would not sneer at the iron, nor the silver challenge the copper; but all would reverently look up to each other, admire each other, compliment each other, and rejoice together in the rich bounties of the universal Giver. To every person that God has created there is given a special deposit of thought, some valuable mineral that can be found by hard, by serious, and by mighty labor, and something that the world needs for its full development; and, when we attempt to cast all minds into one mould, we are trying to thwart the gracious, the benevolent, the economical, and the majestic plans of the Almighty.

Send somebody else, do you tell me, to do your thinking? Never. God forbid. Somebody else cannot do it; for that other person has a personal work sufficiently large for a life's work, and it will not do for your work to be done by him, for, if the attempt be made, two persons will be weakened, and the whole world will be bereaved. Think for yourself, O man, O woman, solemnly, deeply, tenderly, enthusiastically, and reverently, looking up as well as inwardly; and then speak out your holy thought, and bless a waiting, a needy, and a thankful world! Hear, of course, what other people have to say. Look on all sides, compare all sides; recognize the gold, the copper, the iron, and the silver; but stand by your own metal, without the quiver of a doubt, with a spiritual audacity, with a glorious meekness, with a mighty faith, and with a holy eloquence, the echoes of which will reach the very gates of heaven. You have an idea, my friend; it has been in your brain for weeks or months or years, careering, boiling, clamoring, eager, impatient, boisterous, chafing under the bonds of captivity, eager to bless a waiting world, and longing for the bars of the prison-doors to be removed. It is an idea all its own, very original, very sparkling, very comprehensive, and very vital. Why, then, let it escape into the keeping of the world, with all earnest prayer to Almighty God. Send it forth on its mission of grace, and let it go to its appointed work. It may be at first unpolished, very rough, somewhat shallow, and tender, and untutored; but so are all babes, when born. Yet time, experience, discipline, and culture will send all impediments out of the way; and your idea will find its right and righteous place forever and ever. Again, the plan of our lives a great many of us are apt to leave to somebody else. What shall we be? What shall we do? What shall we accomplish in the world? What profession take up? How carry out the grand ideas that seethe in the brain? We may think all right. We may tell out our thoughts; and then we may go and live on a lower plane altogether, following not our own appointed career, but walking the path that some other mortal dares to sketch for us. And how many persons by so doing have wrecked their own existence, sent a confusion into a great many places, created a jar among the vibrations of time, and given discordant notes to the "city of our God"! and thus the world gets seemingly jumbled, dislocated, hedged, and calamities upon calamities are sent as the natural punishment for the grave mistake. If one should preach who was ordained for a healer, if one should be a physician who was ordained for a preacher, if the merchant should have been a mechanic, and the mechanic should have been a teacher,— if many are in places where every blow they give hits the wrong mark, not alone do they suffer by failure, by misappreciation, by bitter remorse, but a thousand other people are rifled of their rights, curtailed in their power, fearfully deceived; namely, those unto whom the wrong administration comes, and those who need the one that does harm in one place, but would be a glory, a benediction, and a mighty power in the right place.

Whatever we are ordained to take up, wherever we ought to go, where Almighty God says plainly, Stand, let us not dare to say, "Send somebody else," not only because by thus doing we dishonor God, but also because by our disobedience we throw over ourselves, our families, our neighbors, and the world, a dark, a thick, and a deadly fog that will injure, sadden, poison, and break many needy hearts. For the sake of God, for the sake of ourselves, for the sake of our dear ones, and for the sake of all humanity, let us take up, let us carry forward, let us hold on to and accomplish our own divinely appointed work, willingly, gratefully, patiently, and full of faith, trust, and love.

Once more, how many of our habits, our ways, and our daily deeds are governed by other people! How often we say, We must do as we are told to do by other people, we must be governed by custom, by fashion, by the majority! and we allow that certain things are doubtful, not just right, not according to our real conscience; but we must go with the rest, and let the crowd take the responsibility.

Do not appoint us to establish new habits, to set up better ways, and to break out a new road, but send somebody else, and let us do as others do: let us be one with the great multitude instead of "one with God." Thus we speak or thus we think.

So we suppose that we shall save pain, trouble, a good deal of present inconvenience, and we are saved from rebuking those who are with us by our singular conduct, and we do not wish to be reformers, but conformers, and thus keep up the peace; but, ah! how sadly we are mistaken! If the limb be broken, it may cause a shriek, a pain, and a remonstrance, as one proceeds to make it right, a long, a loud, an earnest protest, day after day; but, at last, what joy, when all is right, and what thanks to the surgeon who persisted in doing what he thought would be best, despite our inconvenience, our restlessness, and our tears! So, if we, right in the face of a large crowd, insist on living according to our best visions, we shall at last lead all people to be governed by their best visions, and thus shall grandly aid toward the building up of the "kingdom of God." We must not desire that somebody else should be sent to give a good example; but we should each one try, according to our best powers, to set a personal example of obedience, harmony, usefulness, and holiness, proving that the monitor within, and not the voices without, will always be our guide, our help, and our benediction.

"Send somebody else." Here, perhaps, comes another thought. One of the grand secrets of success can be found in our willingness to do what we can by ourselves, to take up our special work, to be at hand, ready, and earnest about our own concerns, and not for a moment to suppose that anybody else can advance our interests any better than we can advance them by our own efforts; that is, as long as we are engaged in any business whatsoever, it will never be safe to leave the whole management of that business to other people. For no one can feel the same interest in our welfare that we feel, and agents, however good, brave, and honest, are never able to take completely the part of the principal; and, if we want anything done, well done, and done to our full satisfaction, in nine cases out of ten, we must do it with our own hands.

You will send somebody else, do you tell me, to make your purchases, to plan your sales, to attend to your business, to do your whole work, and you spend your time for years here, there, and everywhere, with no knowledge whatsoever of your own concerns. Oh, I beseech of you, change your mind, alter your plan, and be governed by more profitable laws; for nobody can strike ten in any concern whatsoever, who puts the work, the responsibility, and the thinking upon "somebody else."

Our Lord and Master did not say, did not want to

say, and never would have thought of saying, "Send somebody else"; and, if he had said that, who, oh, who could have taken his place, who could have set his example, taught his precepts, endured his sufferings, died on his cross, and rose again, like him, for our justification? Do you not feel, as you read his life, all parts of it,— from his birth to his ascension, — that nobody else could have thought as he thought, or planned as he planned, or lived as he lived, or suffered as he suffered, or died as he died, or have risen again like him?

But how grandly he carried forward in every particular the work that he had to do! With all difficulties in his path, he went on conquering and to conquer, with a light in his eye, a grace upon his lips, an elasticity in his steps, a holy power that was sublime beyond all the force of words to describe; and so are we all to go and do likewise. We are told to be like him; but, in one sense, that is not possible. No one's experience can be the exact photograph of another's experience. No one's life can be the perfect copy of another's life. There are no real twin souls, twin brains, twin hearts in the world; for there is always some difference, and the real Jesus can never be duplicated, even if we, for a moment, let alone his divine nature, and look upon him in his earthly career, as "prophet," "priest," and "king."

But, in another sense, we can all be like him: he filled up the full measure of his calling, and so can we fill up the full measure of our calling. A teacup can be filled, and it will be full, and we must call it full, looking at it in the right light; and so can the ocean be full, and both the teacup and the ocean are perfectly filled, according to their ability. If we each one of us do our best, then we are fulfilling all that is demanded of us by our Lord, and, in a certain way, although in a very limited way, we are like him; and, thus doing, we shall grow more and more like him throughout time and throughout all eternity. So may it be, Almighty God!

Ella Wheeler Wilcox says something like this; and with her striking words we will close: —

> "I may not reach the heights I seek:
>   An inborn strength may fail me;
> Or, half way up the mountain peak,
>   Fierce tempests may assail me.
> But, though that place I never gain,
> Herein lies comfort for my pain:
>   I will be worthy of it.

> "I may not triumph in success,
>   Despite my earnest labor:
> I may not grasp results that bless
>   The efforts of my neighbor.
> But, though my goal I never see,
> This thought shall always dwell with me:
>   I will be worthy of it."

VIII.

ILLUSIONS.

"What is your life? A vapor." — ST. JAMES iv. 14.

I DO not know how much the apostle James meant to express by those striking words that we have just quoted, and he undoubtedly had his holy qualifications of the phrase, so that, as he intended that it should be understood, the truth was clear, sound, suggestive, alarming, and beyond a question; and yet, if any uninspired person should say to me, Your life is a vapor, I should impeach the utterance as false to the core, and, in fact, I should say at once that the very words "life" and "vapor" could never coalesce without an explosion, since life can never be vapor, and vapor by no construction can mean life, and neither one has a connection with the other, and both signify the opposite. For, if we are alive, we are not dead and we are not a vapor; and, if we are like vapor, we are not alive, can never be alive, and the whole glory of Christianity rests upon the fact that life never can sink into mist nor fall into nothingness nor leap into a dream, but is forever and ever an eternal reality. Our life, do you tell me, is only a mist? Our life nothing? — a life given to us by Almighty God, filled with sacred possibilities, guarded by angels, surrounded by comforts, flanked by gifts, filled with glory, honor, and beatitudes, bounded by eternity, and ordained to carry out the purposes of Infinite Wisdom! Is such a life all to no purpose? Why, when we say that, we impeach the majesty of eternal goodness, we wipe out all the significance of all the beauties and bounties of nature, we exalt mere materialism into a greater solidity than mortal breath, we throw a satire upon all time, and we deride the benignant gift of immortality. Saint James did not mean, could not mean, did not say, that *spiritual* life was a vapor. What is your life? A vapor. Well, if we say *mortal* life, then the statement is partially correct; although even then there are qualifications, since the poorest life ever lived this side of heaven is something more than a mist, and cannot easily escape responsibility under that convenient phrase.

Perhaps the apostle James did really mean to speak of the tenure of life, the number of years that we spend in the flesh, the short pilgrimage allotted to each one of us, even when we live to a good old age; and that truth we all admit, and every day is the pledge of it. But yet even the shortest life that was ever lived, though it came in the twinkling of an eye and went away from human sight at once, such a life is not a mist, but a reality, and the influence of it goes on here and in heaven forever and ever. I am afraid that, if we content ourselves with looking at our earthly existence as a mere nothing, a smoke, a vision, a dream, a slight spray, we shall probably make nothing of it, and, in fact, we shall naturally suppose that it is hardly worth while for us to trouble ourselves much about that which has so little reality, and which expires almost as soon as it begins; and we shall be inclined to think that there is nothing for mortal to do but to sail listlessly along, without use of the oars, till our life-boat hits the rocks, becomes disabled, and sinks.

We shall say, like the Epicureans, "Let us eat and drink, for to-morrow we die." Why worry? Why weep? Why struggle? Why care? The time is so short, the opportunity so small, the reality so dim, and mere existence such a vapor, why not let the whole life drift as it will, and we take it as easily as we can, doing as we like, thinking what we please, saying what we please, and feeling no moral obligation whatsoever? Certainly, if we make life nothing, there is nothing to do, nothing to bear, nothing to hope. But, if we say that life is an eternal rock, imperishable, responsible, momentous, beginning here, ending nowhere, occupying the body only as a temporary shelter, but having an everlasting body, that cannot be destroyed, if we exclaim, Life is a trust, a hope, a power, a growth, an achievement, and a perpetual glory,— why, then, we find that the very fact that we are now alive constitutes us as trustees forever, and puts us into an employment that cannot end, and marshals into duty our thought, speech, and deed continually, and fastens forever a line of communication between ourselves and Almighty God.

And then it becomes a very solemn reality that we breathe, and that we each one send eternal echoes through earth and heaven. There has been of late a conflict of thought with some persons as to whether, after all, life were worth living. Preachers have announced as their subject this great question about life; but to me the answer seems to have been given by Almighty God himself, at the very instant of our birth, for, by the very fact of our creation, he has announced to all the earth and to all the inhabitants of heaven that life is worth living, that it is a grand reality, a vast responsibility, a holy opportunity, one of his best, choicest, and grandest of gifts. And, if we begin to question life's worth, we throw a cloud over the wisdom of the King of kings, we call in question his justice, we impeach his mercy, we cruelly arraign him as having no insight, no grace, and no holiness. God did not make a mistake when he made the earth and the heavens and all the inhabitants thereof.

Helen Rich said,— and I think by the words she defines the real duty of life, and lifts each day out of vapor into reality: —

"Do the duty nearest,
Cling to truth the clearest,
Face the ill thou fearest,
Hold thine honor dearest,
Knowing God is good.

"Life is worth the living.
What foe withstands forgiving?

Love lives but in believing,
Peace follows after grieving,
And death is only life.

"All good awaits thy earning,
Great souls for light are yearning;
Heaven's lamps are always burning.
Bless God there's no returning
To our dead and buried past!"

As I look at each person that God has created, I am ordered to say, through my commission that is from above, that the very fact that you live is an ordination from Heaven and an installation over a trust that is perpetual; that, by the grace of the Almighty helping, you are put in charge over yourselves, and you must render an account of your stewardship.

Wordsworth says, "Oft in my way have I stood still, though but a casual passenger, so much I felt the awfulness of life"; and Holmes exclaims, "Life, as we call it, is nothing but the edge of the boundless ocean of existence, where it comes upon soundings." And Emerson writes, "What is our life but an endless flight of winged facts or events?" And William Penn tells us, "The truest end of life is to know the life that never ends." And we all remember, I hope, Addison's stirring words,—

"The stars shall fade away, the sun himself grow dim with age,
    and nature sink in years;
But thou shalt flourish in immortal youth,
Unhurt amidst the war of elements,
The wreck of matter, and the crush of worlds."

Thus we see that the greatest minds look upon life as something that cannot be extinguished, cannot float away, and cannot in any way lose its identity, having a birth, but illimitable, immortal, perpetual, responsible, and a grand reality forever.

I know sometimes the anxious father or the troubled mother or the distressed business man, or any one who is for a time unhappy, will, when surrounded by the doubt, difficulty, and danger, exclaim petulantly or sorrowfully or defiantly, "What is the use of life?" But let us not gauge the real opinion of any man, woman, or child, when such are engirdled by deep clouds; for all truth is veiled when the storm is present, and the discontented mood will change with the doubter, when the heavy thunder ceases, when the sharp lightning has gone away, when the fearful showers disappear, for then the sun, full of a blessed light and warmth, will shed a cheerful halo over all creation.

"What is your life? A vapor." Well, Saint James probably meant that what some people call life is only a mist, that wicked people, forgetting life's dignity, power, influence, and perpetuity, make a vapor of it, seemingly fill it with nothing new on its earthly side, or pollute it with sin, or make a mummy of it, or dissolve it in trifles, till its whole history vanishes like smoke, and "Vanity of vanities, all is vanity!" is written upon it, as its record in the body; and yet Saint James would have us remember that, even in the most useless life in the flesh, or in the most corrupt life upon the earth, there is something more than smoke, ashes, vapor, and mist, even a terrible fruitfulness on the sad side and a giving out to the world of poison, day by day and hour by hour. Oh would that some lives could be only mist, soon disappearing, or mingling without hurt with other lives, and losing the poison by a fresh combination, and saved from further harm by the new life and birth! for, if this could only be so ordered, some of the fearful results of wrong-doing would be neutralized and a noxious harvest would be spared. But God has not so ordered it,— at least, for this world; and the wheat and the tares must grow together, and, oh, how frequently the tares spring up and choke the wheat! "What is *your* life? A vapor." Perhaps Saint James, in putting this close question, meant to address each heart that he could then reach, and also wanted to send a message to all hearts that would ever appear through time and through eternity; and it may be that he desired to say to each and all, What are you making of your life? Nothing, or something? Are we working for God, or for self, or for Satan? Or are we going to sleep, and caring not whether the wheat or tares shall grow, and only crying out for a little more sleep and a little more slumber, too lazy to obey God, too selfish to help man, and too careless to bless our own souls?

Then, like vapor, shall our powers vanish, our glory disappear, our good influence leave us, our name be unknown, and our life be blasted,— like vapor, for the talent shall be taken away, and given to somebody else, and other hands shall reap the harvest that might have been ours. Ah, to how many people might we say, with the utmost tenderness, with a great solemnity, with tears, it may be, in our eyes, Think what might have been yours,— a body strong, healthy, and beautiful, a mind sparkling with ideas, rich in depth, and massive in power, a soul full of God, lighted up by fires from heaven, and increasing day by day in holiness, hosts of friends rising up and calling you blessed, cheered by your presence, helped by your counsel, and saved by your giving hand! With a promise, too, all the time, sealed by a celestial bond, of an immortality that can never be impeached! Yes, think what you might have been, and then persistently and penitently think of what you are!

Oh, my friends, how many lives are seemingly wasted on this side of heaven! How many zeroes are found among mortals! how much unreality everywhere! How to all of us, as the English writer beautifully expresses it, "The golden moments in the stream of life rush past us, and we are nothing but sand: the angels come to visit us, and we only know them when they are gone"! How very few are to any degree aware of the responsibility of breath! and how many people, even if they do not throw utterly away their powers, are doing what will amount to the same thing, devoting their lives, their abilities, and their possessions simply to the building up of self, the enthronement of self, and the deification of self, forgetting God, Christ, heaven, and everybody on earth save self, and thus becoming cold, like ice, or hard as lead, or like mummies all the time in the soul! Such lives are not as good as vapor; for vapor will go somewhere and help something, and forget itself, and somehow bless the world. But how shall we escape out of the misty life? For this is the mighty question, after all. Only by obeying the precepts of Jesus, and being helped by the spirit of God, through his Son, day by day and hour by hour; and Mrs. Annie S. Hawks had it right when she said: —

> "I need thee every hour,
> Most gracious Lord!
> No tender voice like thine
> Can peace afford.
>
> "I need thee every hour:
> Stay thou near by.
> Temptations lose their power
> When thou art nigh.
>
> "I need thee every hour:
> Teach me thy will,
> And thy rich promises
> In me fulfil."

Certainly, the older we grow and the more we see of life and take an active part in the doings of the world, the more and the more are we startled by the apparent instability of events, the thousand and one fluctuations of each year, the sudden changes not to be foreseen or understood, or even managed, that greet mortals continually; and everything appears to be built upon a mist, or a vapor, or a dream, and human hopes, plans, and deeds seem to find no place where they can establish an anchor, and all things appear to float into insecurity and nothingness. Yet we are fearfully deceived if we call that which seems just what it seems; and, if we become thoroughly consecrated men and women, we shall find that there is a foundation, and that the Builder and Maker is God. Let us repeat it again and again. A sure trust in God, an unwavering faith in the teachings of the Lord Jesus Christ, a constant sense of the perpetual presence of the Holy Spirit, alone will save us from despair, only will place our feet upon the Everlasting Rock, and will make earth not a vapor and life not a mist and deeds not a dream, but will prove that underneath us, underneath mind, heart, soul, and body are the Rod, the Staff, and the Rock. When we can say that we are children of God and disciples of Jesus, and travellers toward heaven, then delusion will be gone, and reality will have an eternal birth, and we shall find that all things are working together for good to all souls that are in harmony with the Infinite Will. We shall then confess that real life is not a "vapor," but a perpetual power, whose boundary lines eternal ages alone can enclose, and whose possible glory only the great King of kings can fully describe.

IX.

THE CORONATION OF FAILURE.

"Thou shalt not go over." — DEUT. xxxiv. (part 4).

MOSES had a sight of all the blessings that he desired, — of the victories towards which his anxieties, labors, suffering, and prayers had turned, — and he looked at the goodly land where he supposed that he should be the champion to lead his people; and then he was told — oh bitter disappointment, oh sad trial, oh tremendous punishment, oh heavy shame, oh deep and tantalizing and overwhelming pain!— was told, right before the beauty, the glory, and in face of the transcendently happy prospect, "Thou shalt not go over."

Perhaps at first sight, with transient thought, with excited heart, with wild imagination, with reverence, devotion, and holiness in abeyance, we might exclaim, Where was the need of his seeing that which he could not obtain? Why was he not allowed to die without the prospect? Why was it said to him, Look, drink in the view, go into raptures, and then right before him thrown the curtain of despair, the drapery of impossibility, and the everlasting exclusion? My friends, we must remember that Moses was denied his great privilege because he had not carried out the will of God to its full extent, because he had failed to obey all the divine commands, because he had placed his own weak will, at times and very many times, against the better will of Almighty God; and now it was necessary for him to see what he had lost. by his disobedience, — how into other hands must pass the rewards that his own hands had let slip, how neglect of duty must of necessity bring the deprivation of pleasure, and how no life can do as it may please and yet have all that it wants; but still, although the punishment was great, it had its blessed, holy, and glorious alleviations. His people, or their successors, that he had loved so dearly, served so long, and pleaded for so disinterestedly, were not to be set aside; his work was not to come to naught; his plans were not to be frustrated; his struggles, anxieties, pains, and agonies were to have a fruitage in the joy of those for whom his soul had writhed: only he himself, and a few others on the earthly side, were to be excluded, shut down, shut out, denied, and dismissed without the prize.

On the earthly side he paid the penalty, and here is a great thought: he, after acknowledging his sins and giving himself to God, was to pass on to a better work; he was to be lifted to a truer discipline; he was to be promoted to a more joyous service and summoned to a real Canaan, to the pardon, the cleansing, and the coronation of Almighty God. Only one side of his nature was debarred, stricken, mortified, and marked a failure; but his real life was let alone, undisturbed, forgiven, and blessed. And this scene is a grand photograph of the experience of us all, and a little reflection upon it and a cordial application of it will do none of us any harm. "Thou shalt not go over." Well, we all, like Moses, have plans of life, — good or bad or indifferent, — created by the imagination or by the judgment, or by both, fostered with great care, watched over with deep anxiety, carried forward with enthusiasm, prayed over constantly, harrowing mind and heart, using up days and nights and years, — the one sole purpose of our will, the great, the absorbing, the all-controlling, and the tremendous dream of our earthly lives, to which we dedicate our hands, our time, everything that we have, and towards the accomplishment of which we rapidly approach, — dreams, plans, visions, that seem almost to have their blessed fulfilment, the fruits of which are dropping into our hands, ripe, attractive, and splendid, when it is said, "Thou shalt not go over," and the vision vanishes, and the great work of our lives is shattered, despoiled, and upset.

Then what protests, what sighs, what groans, what rebellion, and what utter discontent and despair! We do not hear that Moses said a word: he took his doom in silence; he did not lift up his finger to object; he went to his fate with resignation, peace, and a perfect submission. But with us how often it is otherwise! We forget our God, we deny our Redeemer, we cover ourselves with sackcloth and ashes, and our whole nature is poisoned, disabled, and upset; and yet, like Moses, we have our compensations, if we will only look at them, weigh them, appropriate them, and glorify them.

It is something that we have marched right up to a victory, close up to it, within the borders of it, even if we have not grasped it; for that we have gone so far is really a solid proof, a very strong indorsement, a sure expression, and a mighty hint of great labors heroically endured, of large sufferings splendidly met, of daring aspirations bravely nurtured, such as only a resolute mind, a stalwart soul, and an active hand could possibly display. Nay, to have reached the very verge of accomplishment is a great accomplishment of itself, and proves, indeed, very many superior qualities of character, so that even just missing the mark is a sign of a man of mark, or of a woman of mark, or of a child of wonderful powers; and losing the prize is not always the terrible thing that many so thoughtlessly consider it.

You tell me that he or she failed, that they almost reached the point desired, and then dropped, hampered by sickness, conquered by suffering, smothered by overwork, or chilled by death; and you add, What a cruel shame, what an untimely dispensation, what a fearful loss! I say, Look on the other side, give credit for what has been done, and do not mark zero on all the steps gained, do not call a blank the acquired powers, do not thrust into obscurity that which has been almost a success and thank God that the disappointed ones did so well as far as they went, which is very much better in a good effort than if they had never started in the race. Many persons to-day worship success, altogether too much, label success as the real possession of the prize, and forget all about the spiritual diamonds, pearls, and rubies that are picked up all along on the road to victory. The seemingly disappointed ones may not have obtained that for which they aimed; but in the very efforts that they have made they may have reached a maturity of character that is surprising, charming, and glorious.

Again, it is a great thing to be allowed to stand on Mt. Nebo and to look at the promised land; for the next thing to having is gazing, and gazing is freed from all the responsibility of possession. If we cannot go to Europe, we can obtain the most perfect photographs of all the leading cities, the splendid monuments, the glorious paintings, the massive buildings, and all things beautiful, grand, and striking; and we can do all this without being sick at sea, without paying large bills, without fatigue, depression, and loss of much time, so that next to going abroad is a good, a long, a loving, a happy, a genial, and an inspiring look at pictures of the other side of the world.

If we cannot own a glorious estate, with its ponds, its parks, its statues, its conservatories, and all its beauties, we have eyes that can see it, a soul that can appreciate it, and lungs that can breathe its pure air, without paying the taxes on it, and without enduring the thousand worries in the care of it.

Yes, it is a great privilege to look at a prize, even although it may never be ours; for it is surely ours, if we are in the true mood, by sight, insight, faith, trust, and love, in the true mood to appreciate, measure, and appropriate it.

Yes, we may own the world if we only have a heart large enough to take in the world, and to make it ours through taste, through imagination, and through holy appreciation.

Of course, to what we have said there must be some decided qualifications. If, like Moses, we have failed of our victory because we have disobeyed God's laws, then in the sight of the prize we certainly are filled with remorse, grief, and disappointment; and yet, even then, I maintain, we ought to thank God for the glimpse of what we might have been. In one of our albums of characters, where each one writes a reply to certain questions that are stated, this answer is given to the query, "What are the saddest words?" — namely, "It might have been."

In one sense it was a good reply, but in a higher sense it was a mistake; for I maintain that what might be, although it never has been, is one of the massive seals to God's great goodness, one of the best pledges of our own possible royalty, one of the glorious proofs of our immortality, one of the holy testimonies for eternity. For, if we have a possible, who is to stop us from some day reaching it? What we cannot do here may we not do somewhere, and is not the possible a grand excelsior cry to all humanity and the bugle-note that should stir up all hearts?

When Moses went up the mountain of Nebo, at the top of Pisgah, looked at Gilead, Dan, Naphtali, Ephraim, Manasseh, Judah, and Jericho, and Zoar, almost in his hand, and yet never to be really his property, I think that what might have been, although a deprivation, was yet a glory: it was the full bursting out of the possible grandeur that mere human beings could obtain by a strict obedience to the will of Almighty God.

I wonder what sort of a biography might be written of each one of us if we only were to-day what we all might have been. Might have been if we had only just turned a different corner, just kept down a hasty word, just been true to our best impulses, just put aside a great temptation, just practised a little self-restraint, just had a little more courage; if we had curbed our ambition or smothered our pride or cleansed our imagination; if only some little thing had been different; if our parents had not met with misfortune or had not passed away when we needed their advice; if husband or wife had been just the opposite to what they are, or children or brothers or sisters had taken a different course, what we might have been. Again, I say, look on the other side. Thank God through our Lord Jesus for what you have gained, for the strength that has come through deprivation, for the mere outlook upon what might have been. So, my friends, with us all, as we look from Nebo upon rewards not ours, it is something, it is a great deal, it is a magnificent glory, that they might have been ours; and it is a hint of what may yet be ours if, through a true penitence, a holy resignation, a divine peace, we bow before the ordinances of the Eternal God. This leads us to the thought that we would repeat again and again,— that, although Moses did not get the grand prize that bathed his eyes, he yet, by true penitence, obtained something better: he fell asleep, and entered the "City of the New Jerusalem," the promised land for all consecrated souls.

So with all mortals: we may not get what we want, what we expect, that for which we have diligently worked,— may not reach the height of our ambition, the dream of our life, the aim of all our hopes, and our life vision may vanish; yet we may, by giving ourselves up to God, attain unto something much more grand. The earthly Canaan may fade away; but the heavenly Canaan is at hand, where no disappointment comes, where no pain is felt, where all agony is finished, where all growth is possible, and where all joy is without limit. Moses went to God; and thus his struggles were ended, his trials were finished, his responsibility was closed, and his real victory was attained. And so all consecrated lives that go to God have reached the victory, although the earthly record may seem unfinished, rough, and strangely mixed up or broken off at the moment of a beautiful completion, and other hands may reap the fruits that seemingly belonged to those who have gone away.

This brings us to a very important part of what ought to be called one of the blessings of Moses: that he, the prophet, was able to know that his work was not really in vain; that he was assured that his people or their successors should finally obtain all the rewards, the comforts, the peace, the honors, the victories, and the gains for which he had in their behalf prayed, struggled, and worked; that, although he failed to reach his earthly mark, his loved ones, or their children or their children's children, should be benefited; and he could say, with a sweet comfort, a holy peace, and a joyous exultation, My labors are not lost.

Thus, my friends, can we in a like situation rejoice for this holy land before our prospect shall belong to somebody and, it may be, come into the hands of those that we love: we may fail, but they shall endure; we may drop the oars, but somebody else shall pick them up, and there shall be a final triumph. And this fact is the real glorification of all work; for every blow tells, every pain has an echo, and all good things shall have a plenteous harvest. Blessed be God! What matter whether you or I pick up the results of our endeavors, reap the advantages of our prayers, are crowned as victors in the battle, if we are only the pioneers to victory, if we only clear the way, open the road, knock down the obstructions, and make it easier for somebody else?

A zero by itself is not much; but a zero in its proper place, doing its right work, patiently maintaining its position, helps make ten, helps make one hundred, helps to make an infinity of numbers, and, although the zero may never take the prize by itself, some of the figures that it has helped will take the prize, and all owing to what that poor, little, and insignificant zero has accomplished./ So, in this way of looking at the matter, we may be sure that no true soul ever fails, that every noble effort tells, and that victory somewhere is the sure award of a consecrated toil.

"Thou shalt not go over." Did we ever stop to think that not one of those noble men who signed the Declaration of Independence ever went over to the full possession of the grand results of which their daring signatures were the precious seed that was cast into the ground?

Of course, they lived to see their country acknowledged by the other Powers in the world; they came under the canopy of the stately recognition of the hesitating, critical, and irritable King of England; they marched into the full splendor of a government established and in working order; they beheld thirteen States interlocking arms and bowing to a central Power that was but faintly understood. But they lived only long enough to bask in the twilight of the grandeur that was to come. They had no panorama of the United States of to-day: they could hardly have dreamed of the present power and wealth and culture of the nation at this hour,— a nation whose flag is respected in every country and whose scholarship and statesmanship and acquired authority call out the admiration and the respect of the world.

Take the photograph of our country as the United States looked when the Declaration of Independence was signed, and close to it place the photograph of the United States as they appear to-day; and the contrast will be sublime.

Now look at our Master. If we judge his work on the earthly side, merely by human measurement, according to the laws of a strictly mathematical reputation, as such life has within its circumference only the three years of active manhood, we shall have to exclaim, His plans failed, his labors were cut off, all his exertions faded into thin air; and, instead of the crown that he deserved, he had to take a cross. Well, if our vision be limited to three years only,— to the Holy Land for that time and to ancient records alone of that day,— our judgment, however sad, is true. But, thanks be to Almighty God, although Jesus Christ did not pass over to the acceptance of the Jews and to the welcome of the Romans, did not conquer the world in his own day, did not obtain the high honors that he deserved in the temple,— only had a view from Pisgah,— yet the reward came, the glory was sure, the conquest grand; and, measured by the circuit of eternity, he becomes the appointed Head, Judge, and Redeemer of the world. And his life teaches us that we are not to measure our lives by minutes, hours, and days, but by revolving centuries and by eternal years.

Sears says: —

"O bright ideals, how ye shine,
  Aloft in realms of air!
Ye pour your streams of light divine
  Above our low despair.
I've climbed and climbed these weary years,
  To come your glories nigh.
I'm tired of climbing, and in tears
  Here on the earth I lie.

"Ah! this one thought of hope and trust
  Comes with its soothing balm,
As here I lay my brow in dust,
  And breathe my lowly psalm,—
That not for heights of victory won,
  But those I tried to gain,
Will come my gracious Lord's 'Well done!'
  And sweet, effacing rain."

X.

DISCONTENT.

"Oh that I had wings like a dove." — Ps. lv. 6.

THE Psalmist wanted to get into a better place and into a higher place, and into a locality outside of temptation, care, and struggle, where he could grow, grow fast, have no pullbacks, and feel himself rising, rising, and forever rising up to Almighty God. Well, it was a natural feeling for him to indulge, and one which falls into some of our moods to-day; and I would not interpret it, as some do, as wholly weariness on his part. But I would call it an aspiration for a higher level; for, in events, opportunities, and achievements, we would all of us like to fly, if we could, into certainty, victory, peace, and glory.

Some feel at times that life is terribly tame, the harp of experience giving its music all on one string, and duty fastened to one groove, expectation running into well-known paths, and everything marked out instead of being forced out or thrust unexpectedly upon us. Ella Wheeler Wilcox says something like this:—

"The current of life runs ever away
   To the bosom of God's great ocean.
Don't set your force 'gainst the river's course,
   And think to alter its motion.
Don't waste a curse on the universe,
   Remember it lived before you.
Don't push at the storm with your puny form,
   But bend and let it go o'er you.

"The whole will never adjust itself
   To suit your whims to the letter.
Some things must go wrong your whole life long;
   And the sooner you know it, the better.
It is folly to fight with the Infinite
   And go under at last in the wrestle.
The wise man shapes into God's plan,
   And close unto God's goodness will nestle."

But still the student wants to be in Athens, the dreaming girl at the court of Queen Elizabeth, the martial spirit back in the crusades; and a great many want to be anywhere but where they are, because where they are seems like the same tread in the mill all the time. To a certain extent this dissatisfaction, this sense of unrest, and this dreadful sensitiveness are promising, healthy, and prophetic; for the one who is not content with the present will perhaps make a time, by the grace of Almighty God, that shall be holy, bright, and beautiful, and such a one will force blessedness out of the future. That we are not satisfied is sometimes a great thing; for then our ideas are quickened, our reason is purified, our judgment is cleansed, and our whole nature is elevated, strengthened, and redeemed.

Aspiration, when it keeps aloof from ambition, frees itself from pride, abstains from vain and empty desire, and allies itself to the will of Almighty God, is that which makes every man, woman, and child better, holier, safer, and is the power that regenerates the world.

Why, without aspiration, dreaming, impatient desire, and holy determination, the world would go back to the days of Genesis, and all the glory of to-day would be lost. Yet, sometimes, when we long for wings to circumstances, we ought to be satisfied with things as they are; for excitement, novelty, and tremendous changes, without a pause, would be a heavy curse to the race,— wiping out all observation, putting an end to established facts, and making life like a throw of dice or a game of chance,— haphazard, uncertain, and balanced all the time on volcanoes and on earthquakes that are terrible to conceive. There must be in this life a great deal of calm, steady effort and slow progress, in order that, when the storm comes, it may be appreciated; for, if it were always stormy weather, real growth would cease, signal lights would be of no avail, harbor lines would be dashed away, and navigation would end. Do you tell me, young man and young woman, that your life is tame, that you see nothing grand in life, that day after day and week after week you hear the same sounds, do the same things, seemingly bring nothing to pass, and that you long for something, even a tempest, if the routine could be only broken and a new turn given to the tide of your destiny? Ah! my friends, you are craving a terrible gift that you will not be able to bear. You greatly misunderstand and underrate your present ability, and you make altogether too little of that which you now possess. For action is not to be developed from without, but from within; and our growth is silently going on in the soul from seeds that are planted by the grace of the Almighty.

But I am ready to admit that wings are very convenient if we only know how to use them; but we must remember that not one in a thousand, if they had wings, could fly: they would only flutter and flutter, and then they would fall to the ground utterly exhausted.

With mortals the law is very different from what it is with the birds. A bird, in a very little while, by instinct, learns to sail in the air with great beauty, — perhaps aided at first by maternal solicitude; but in mortal beings the real force, the true struggle, and the mighty energy must be inward, or else all the outward wings in the world will be of no possible avail. Ah! there must be wings to the soul and to the heart and to the mind, or we can never fly.

Have you not read the words of some of our great thinkers concerning action? Hear what a few of the best minds say. Whittier exclaims, "Speak out in acts: the time for words is passed, and deeds alone suffice." Adam Clarke writes, "I have lived to know that the secret of happiness is never to allow your energies to stagnate." And the great writer of England tells us, "Let us take the instant by the forward top; for we are old, and over our quickest decrees the inaudible and noiseless foot of time steals ere we can effect them." Ah! my friends, to a great extent we must make our excitements, create our surprises, and cause the hours of the day to scintillate with honor and with glory; for it is only as we strike the iron at white heat that we can bend it to our best will.

Longfellow says: —

> "We have not wings, we cannot soar;
> But we have feet to scale and climb
> By slow degrees, by more and more,
> The cloudy summits of our time.

> "The heights by great men reached and kept
> Were not attained by sudden flight;
> But they, while their companions slept,
> Were toiling upward in the night."

This brings us to our second point, — that the wings of opportunity are desired, and yet, by the brave spirit, they are made almost out of nothing. I have no chance, say many a man and many a woman: only give me the chance, and I will be a hero or a heroine, and the echoes of my deeds shall bound down the generations. No chance! Ah! you are wofully deceived; for you have the same right of way as Galileo or Copernicus or Columbus or Webster or

Everett, or as any of the great men and women that have lighted up the centuries. And all you have to do is to open your eyes, unstop your ears, brace up your soul, stretch out your hands, and give up despair; and then your time will come.

Oh that you had wings! Why, you have wings, if you will only see them; and all you have to do is to look them up, to put them on, and to use them. "Take," says one, "all the swift advantage of the hours"; and still another eloquently cries out, "The best men are not those who have waited for chances, but who have taken them,— besieged the chance, conquered the chance, and made the chance their servitor." All that we need is to be up and doing, with a clear head, with a warm soul, with an earnest endeavor, and all will be well.

Sitting still, grumbling, and Micawber-like "waiting for something to turn up," will amount to nothing; but we must arise and go hence,— go to our duty, march to our destiny, and bring about a glorious victory.

Again, we wish that our achievements had more wings; that is, we want whatever we do to be more widely known, and we want all the time to be doing something that shall make a report here and always. Well, perhaps that which we are now doing, mean as it seems to us,— lowly, obscured, quiet, and dull,— perhaps that, even that, is now sounding a glorious report in the City of the New Jerusalem. Yes, that, even that, is forming gradually the golden wings that will be given to us as we enter heaven; and we shall discover that what we thought little was mighty, beautiful, and transcendently glorious before all the angels of God.

There is a beautiful legend connected with the site on which the temple of Solomon was erected. It is said to have been occupied in common by two brothers, one of whom had a family; but the other had none. On the spot was a field of wheat. On the evening succeeding the harvest the wheat, having been gathered in sheaves, the elder brother said to his wife: "My younger brother is unable to bear the burden of the heat of the day. I will arise, take off a part of my shocks, and place them with his, without his knowledge." The younger brother, being actuated by the same benevolent motives, said within himself: "My elder brother has a family, and I have none. I will contribute to their support. I will arise, take off a part of my shocks, and place them with his, without his knowledge." Judge of their astonishment, when, on the following morning, they found that their respective shocks were undiminished. This course of events transpired for several nights, when each resolved in his own mind to stand guard, and, if possible, solve the mystery. They did so, when, on the following night, they met each other half-way between their respective shocks, with their arms full. Now, neither of these brothers thought much of the deed that was done; yet up in heaven such a thing is recorded, and there it will shine more and more unto the perfect day. If what we do to-day be done from a right spirit, from a holy motive, and with an earnest purpose, without complaint and without rest, as due to God, Christ, and man, it cannot be small, it can never be wholly concealed, and it is filled with glory, honor, power, beauty, and redemption.

Do not tell me that you are doing nothing, that you are of no account in this great world, and that your life is a failure; for, if you are doing all that you can do, the reverberation of your deeds will roll with a splendid beauty throughout eternal ages. And, if you are not doing what you are perfectly able to do, why, then, wake up at once and do better, and fill out the full measure of your high calling. But, by all means, never stand still disconsolate, disheartened, and fearfully cast down, crying out perpetually for wings; but just take the wings that are right before you, and put them on and fly. Some people want to get away from the place where they are, and so they cry out for "wings"; but, unless they can get into God's kingdom, are they sure that the change will do them any good, and will they not find troubles anywhere and everywhere? Then, again, while they are in this discontented state, are they really quite ready for heaven? Will not their distrust of God cast a shade somewhat upon their white robes? I know that we are all apt to think that we should have been better, and that we should have done better, if God had only placed us somewhere else, or if he could only now just change our situation. No such thing! We are very much mistaken; for we can be heroes and heroines where we are, and we can take up our red-hot balls of discipline, and, by a tremendous exertion, by a chemical application, and by the mighty grace of God, we can change them into spiritual rubies, diamonds, pearls, and everything beautiful. What we really want is a fresh baptism of the Holy Spirit, and then we can gain the "wings" that are made of faith, trust, love, and a deep and an unswerving devotion.

"Oh that I had wings like a dove!" I suppose that the dove would say, could it only speak, "Oh that I had feet just like the feet of a man!" and then I would accomplish something great and good, and I would move the world. Poor dove! It has wings, and it wants feet. Poor man! He has feet, and he wants wings. Each is craving what the other has, when both, by making the best use of what is given, will rise to a true glory.

But the dove, better than the man, does its level best, and acts out its full nature.

So let it be with us! It is not necessary for us to fly; but it is necessary for us to walk on steadily through life, turning neither to the right nor to the left, keeping an eye upon God, holding the hand of Christ, and helping in all ways our fellow-men. And we should be forever assured that the least we can do is great if glorified by Heaven.

Near the rocky harbor of New York a little babe

touched the key by which an explosion occurred that shook the city and freed the sea of encumbrances and injured no one.

So even a babe may do wonders.

One has thus beautifully told the story: —

> "A touch of a baby's finger,
> And the awful force outleapt,
> And crumbled the granite mountain
> That the swelling seas o'erswept.
>
> "At touch of a baby's finger
> Many a heart of rock,
> Whelmed in the bitterest of waters,
> Parts as to earthquake's shock.
>
> "The *ancient* bowlder burst
> 'Neath the touch of the prophet's rod,
> But the touch of a baby's finger
> Is the force that is nearest God."

But, my friends, do not think that I have not spoken enough, all the time that I have been speaking, about the grace of God, the love of the blessed Redeemer, the outpouring of the Holy Spirit, and the help which alone prevails that comes down from Heaven. Do not think I for a moment believe that any man, by his own unaided strength, can climb to success, master the world, and attain eternal glory; that any dreams or exertion or consecration will be triumphant without the rod and staff of the Almighty. Oh, no! The wings of the dove will avail nothing, unless those wings are filled, uplifted, and glorified by the gales that are sent from the celestial city; and, when those gales are sent, the tiniest power will send its report through time and through eternity. When we become children of God, disciples of Jesus, and cleansed by the Holy Ghost, we can do all needed things, attain all gracious success, and receive at least the crown that is prepared for us above. Glory be to God!

XI.

LOOKING TO THE FUTURE.

"I will fetch my knowledge from afar."—JOB xxxvi. 3.

IT is a great thing to understand the past, it is a still greater thing to weigh rightly the present; but it is the mark of the best wisdom when we can see "afar off," when the experience of the past and the discipline of the present, by the aid of a wise and a holy mind and soul, can give to one a map of the future so lighted up that no day will be a surprise, but that all days will be rightly met, conquered, and glorified.

Historians are useful, diary writers are important, but seers are best of all; for they take hold of history and grasp the events of to-day, and thus get a chart for all days, for all time, and for all eternity. The old sayings, "What has been will be" and "There is no new thing under the sun," although so often repeated, commended, and looked upon as the truest philosophy, are only the birth of lazy thinking, of seared affections, and of a stunted soul; for the real spiritual hero or heroine believes in growth, and in a growth that has a law, a root, a trunk, a stem, and a flower, but no root, no trunk, no stem, and no flower precisely like any other.

"I will fetch my knowledge from afar."

I am aware that a great many writers insist upon it that it is not well to see afar off; that we are to live by the day, and not by the years; that long views are a mistake; that burrowing into coming hours is an impertinence; and that thinking of anything but the present duty is a folly not approved and a crime before God. And such quote for their authority the words that certainly at first sight seem to be unanswerable, "Sufficient unto the day is the evil thereof"; "Take no thought for the morrow, for the morrow will take thought for itself"; and yet these words, rightly understood, will be found to be only a protest against undue anxiety, and are no anathema against a prudent foresight, since, in another place of Holy Writ, it is said, "Gather up the fragments that remain, that nothing be lost"; and that certainly means, Look ahead and provide for contingencies. We must, then, all of us, to a certain extent, look "afar off,"—the boy or the girl to the time when manhood or womanhood will come; the young man or the woman to the time of mid-life; those in mid-life to the time of old age; and all to the kingdom of God, where all true souls shall be gathered.

Let us look at this matter a little closely. I know very well the old sayings, Be a boy while you are a boy, be a girl while you are a girl; and stop looking afar off into that manhood and womanhood which will be well enough when revealed, but are not now to be the matter of a thought or a dream or a wish. And there is a wisdom, to a certain extent, in such thoughts as these; for what is the use of being troubled about the roof of a house before the cornerstone is laid, or why should we talk about the steeple of a church before the ground is dug on which that church is to be built? There is a great deal of anticipation that is a heavy clog to the wheels of progress, that excites the mind unduly, that casts a cloud upon the heart, that will send a paralysis to effort, upset all discipline, and vitiate all culture. In fact, I think that half of those whom we call our stunted men and women came to that disaster by playing the game of men and women years before the right time, and by usurping an authority that was never conferred by God or by man. And the most rebellious children at home and disobedient pupils at school are those who in their childhood pretend to be full grown; for such, feeling that they know everything, have very little that they can learn, and they rebel against order, studies, and everything except their own sweet will. But, after making all these concessions, I still insist upon it that boys or girls must look "afar off"; and only as they do so look will they rightly attain their true growth.

The posture of the mind and the soul seems to me to be just this, if expressed in words: "I am a boy or I am a girl with much to learn, with many faults, subject to improvement, advice, and correction in the preliminary stage of formation; but I shall be, before many years, a man or a woman,— a free agent, acknowledged by the law as a personality freed from all guardianship, responsible to myself, to the community, and to God, for myself and my doings; and now I must get thoroughly prepared for life's grand apocalypse." And the difference between the false looking ahead and the true gaze is really expressed under the two words "assumption" and "consecration."

The young person that assumes, dictates, and puts on airs, becomes an offence, sends a jar to the heart, and calls out our righteous indignation; but the young person that is truly consecrated, while looking at the days that are to come, is humble, docile, patient, serious, and calls out our deepest love.

Again, the young man or woman must look forward to the time when life will be half spent,— when the eye sees not so well, the ear hears not so quickly, motion is not quite so vigorous, nor imagination quite so glowing, when judgment is ripened and hope somewhat depressed.

It would not do for young men and women to feel that youth is a perpetuity, that strength can never fail, and that all things are just as they seem. I know that a great many persons say: Let the delusion go on till a crash shall come. Let a sharp experience, the best master of all, be the first revealer of the changes of life. Never let anticipation be clouded, nor dreams be broken, nor the blue sky eclipsed; but, from twenty-one to forty, let every one, of all sexes, build their castles in the air without a protest or a challenge or a denial. And, to some extent, the advice is good.

Take a peach-tree full of blossoms, and suppose that it could understand the human voice, what would be the use of saying to it: A great many of your blossoms will fall to the ground, and some of the peaches that will be given to you will be hard, and but very little of your fruit will be worth possessing? No, no! Let the peach-tree go on, and do what it can, and learn by time its life of gains or failures; but yet, could we not say to that peach-tree, Your blossoms are beautiful and fragrant: they anoint the air, they charm the eye, and they bless the heart. And now do what you can to turn all your promises into performance; but do not be discouraged if a part of your plan be broken, for the glory of the holiest growth comes through self-sacrifice, and we must all do our best and leave results to the appointment of a power wiser than our own. But change the peach-tree into a young man or woman, and would it not be better that such a one in this way should glorify the future?

Again, those in mid-life must consider the time of old age. I am aware that this time is often looked upon with great reluctance, shame, and agony; as inevitable, but a curse; as a doom, but a tragedy; as a dark cloud rising in the distance. And in no such way as this would I lead your thoughts; for I never could conceive how so many shrink back from increasing years, and try to forget and make others forget that they are at hand, and sometimes deny the time that has been passed by them, and cling to an assumed youth as a positive benediction. No, no! I never could understand this hanging back; for all through my own life I have looked forward to old age with delight, have welcomed it in advance, have almost challenged it to approach, have seen its manifold blessings and have placed out of sight all its accompanying weaknesses, and have said to myself, How beautiful it will be when I shall become old, when I shall be counted among the patriarchs, when I shall look back over a long vista of years, and look forward to the eternal years that are so near and so blessed! Not that I have wished for any longer life than the good Father desired to give to me; but I have made up my mind simply that old age, were it given, would be a benediction,— of course, if given with a moderate amount of health, with a clear mind, and with shelter and food sufficient for the support and the comfort of the body. But all these material comforts should be left cheerfully to the will of God. But, again, I say all, in the true way, should consider the time of old age that may come, and should make provisions for the same, that body, mind, and soul may then be reasonably comfortable, happy, and full of peace.

Let us not spend our strength too fast, for it may be wanted as a reserve. Let us not starve our mind; for by and by good thoughts will be a help, when eyesight fails and friends are but few. Let us build up a Christian character, and feed the soul with righteousness by the grace of God; for there may be a future for us in this earth when our only support will be our faith, our only comfort our prayers, and our only glory our consecration.

Ay, in this way we all should so look afar off, and prepare for that which is coming.

I may be old, said one to me, and I am saving a little ahead in case that time should come; for I do not want to be a burden to anybody. And he was right; and we all should carry this rule out in all directions, and put by a supply, financial, physical, mental, and spiritual. And, then, we shall never be taken by surprise, and can always stand up, God and Christ helping us.

Finally, friends, we must all look afar off to the kingdom of God, where at last all faithful souls will be gathered. There is such a thing as dwelling too much upon heaven, so that the duties at hand are put aside, forgotten, and despised; for it is a solemn fact that, while we live upon the earth, we must pay some attention to the duties of every day. Otherwise, our real spiritual life will be terribly discrowned.

He who will not care for himself and for his family, said the holy writer, is worse than an infidel; and there are a great many people who justify their neglect of home and business on the grounds that they must give their whole time to the Church and to Heaven, but they make a sad mistake.

We have our duties to God, and they must not be

forgotten; but also we have our obligations to each other and to ourselves,— obligations that Almighty God himself has imposed upon us,— and he, the Infinite One, will call us to account if, on the ground of extra holiness, we ignore the work of life. Yet the trouble is not so much with those who think too much of spiritual matters and of eternal realities as it is with those who give but very little thought, if any, to anything of the kind. We must look afar off, into the City of God, where we shall some day go; and it would be very sad indeed if we were found there without the wedding garment. In fact, the great rule for all of us may be condensed in a very few words; namely, prepare for manhood or womanhood, prepare for mid-life, prepare for old age, prepare for heaven; and pray to God, through Jesus Christ, all the time, for help in the great work.

"I will fetch my knowledge from afar," said the writer of old. There is a seeing into the distance, a weighing of the future, a calculation as to how things will turn out, eminently wise, prudent, and safe. In fact, all education, all prosperity, and all future success depend not only in clearly understanding the past, in hopefully measuring the present, but in a forecasting of the future that makes all allowances for probabilities and for possibilities, an on-looking that is not carried away by a big hope nor by a wild expectation nor by an unbalanced enthusiasm, but that is cheered, fortified, and consecrated by a firm faith in God and by a wise measurement of human nature.

It is not safe to expect too much: on the one hand, we must not let our imagination run away with us; on the other hand, we must not let our forebodings paralyze our efforts. Of course, we cannot see what is afar off; but we can prepare to meet what comes. We can rightly know our own powers and circumstances, so that we may really feel sure that we are ready for anything and for everything that may be sent to salute us.

We cannot outline our future career, we cannot take our instrument and get an exact photograph of all the events that are to greet us year by year. Imagination will avail nothing as a revealer, boasting will amount to nothing as a prophet, and all the promising in the world will explode, unless, with the imagination and with the boasting and with the promising, we have all the time the upward look to God and the onward look to duty; and then we may say, as Job said, "We will fetch our knowledge from afar"; then we may have our faith lighted up all along the line by the grace of God and the approval of our conscience. And then life will be resplendent, consecration will be grand, and victory will be sure.

XII.

TRANSIENT SIGHT OF GOD.

"How little a portion is heard of him!"—JOB xxvi. 14.

SAINT AUGUSTINE had a vision. He found himself trying to write out the exact definition of the Divine Being; and, being troubled about explaining the subject, he took a walk by the seashore, where he noticed a little child taking cups of water from the ocean and pouring the water into a little hole that he had made in the sand. "What are you doing, my child?" said the great preacher. "I am trying to put the whole ocean into this little place." "But that is impossible, my child." "So is it impossible," replied the child, "for you to put the nature of God into your small definitions."

Ah, how little we know about God, Christ, death, heaven, life, time, ourselves, and anything whatsoever! How slight are the hints that are given, how unsatisfactory our researches, how misty our conclusions, how half-shaped our knowledge, how utterly incomplete everything that we say, think, and feel; what a cloud continually upon mind, body, heart, soul, time, and eternity! In our dark moods we call our knowledge glimpses, dreams, fairy tales, guesses, and vapors. Is it so? Tell me, is it really so?

Are we groping continually in the dark, fumbling along with no chart, no compass, no help, no light, no peace, and gaining no results but an "if" or a "perhaps"?

If this be the case, pitiable is the very gift of life, and dreary the very outlook into eternity; and all breath seems to be a sad mistake. Of course, at first, we admit,—we are obliged to admit,—we must accept the verdict that we know but little and very little. How inexpressibly small our knowledge!—a twinkle, a mote, a sunbeam, and a drop; and the unknown is like the ocean, and the saying that the words of our text proclaim is true,—"How little a portion is heard of him!" But yet, brothers, sisters, and friends, children of God, disciples of Christ, and heirs of eternity, how grand is that little,—how far-reaching, how comforting, how holy, how beautiful, how sublime, and how indestructible!

The little that we do know will save us! And the little, if understood, obeyed, and glorified, will bring more knowledge; and by that little every soul can climb to everlasting blessedness by the grace of the dear Father of us all, through our Lord Jesus Christ.

How little we know of Almighty God! True, very true,—sometimes startlingly true! We cannot pierce into the depths of the eternity that belongs to his past history. We cannot measure the power that encircles his present life. We cannot forecast the glory that will fill up his oncoming eternity. We cannot dissect his nature, although some theologians have dared to try the experiment. We cannot describe him as the anatomist describes the human body, and label every part and parcel of his mighty glory. There is no perfect chart that the human can give to us of the Divine, and such a nature is to a great extent an unexplored labyrinth forever. And yet — glory hallelujah! — a faint insight we can all of us gain. How little! but yet a something, — a something that will have an echo, and that little a true benediction. We can find out that God is love, that he is our Father, that in him we live and move and have our being, that he is from everlasting to everlasting, that he is a Judge, that he is too pure to behold iniquity, that he has hidden many things from the wise and prudent and has revealed them unto babes, that he hears and answers prayer, that not a sparrow falls to the ground without his blessed notice, that he orders all things for good to those that love him; and we can find out a thousand other things that will be enough — ay, enough and more than enough — to lift us out of our terrible darkness into a marvellous light.

How little we know of Jesus! say some. Yes; but that little, how great! We know of him as an obedient child, on the mortal side; as a pure and good young man, when he appeared before the world in human garments; as prophet, priest, and king; as Son of God and son of man; as way, truth, and life; as a good shepherd; as the vine; ay, as all that was holy, great, tender, loving, and beautiful; as resigned in suffering, patient in death; as one who conquered death and made immortality sure; as the greatest preacher of all ages and the Redeemer of the world, — human and divine, of earth and of heaven, the Mediator and Lord; and what more do we need?

Describe him fully, do you say? Who can? Tell just his relation to God and his affiliation to man, do you demand? Who is able? But we must love him, obey him, acknowledge him, cling to him, and by him be led to Almighty God. But yet, when we arrive in heaven and see Jesus, how small all our best earthly knowledge will appear, — how inadequate, how weak, how shadowy, how absolutely poor, at the best! For we shall find him so much more than our highest dreams, so much better than our deepest reasonings, so much more beautiful than our most eloquent descriptions, — everything above what everybody has said of him, — that we shall want to go right back to earth to rectify our mistakes, that we may again build up in the human heart a love for Christ; ay, the truest love of all, because spiritual eye has seen, spiritual ear has heard, and spiritual heart conceived, the glory of the risen Lord.

How little we know about death! It comes into our homes, it breaks up the family circle, it puts ice on the heart, it covers us with clouds. We know not what to do, what to say, where to go; we cry out in our agony, in our fear, in our loneliness, that we cannot bear the blow. And yet, if we will see that in all nature death leads to life, — that in all nations, from the earliest time, an eternal death was forever doubted; if we will read the Christian revelation that death is an impossibility,— then our aching hearts will leap up to God in gratitude for the great hope of immortality; and we shall bow before God in lowly submission to his ever holy but mysterious will. How little we know of heaven! So little that many leave the thought of it out of sight altogether, and some try to wipe it away with the huge sponge of denial, and all, or nearly all, or a great many, treat it like a dream or a vision or a very unsubstantial reality,— a beautiful future terribly veiled. And yet, as we analyze the little that we do know, are we not abundantly blessed?

"In our Father's house are many mansions."

Then there will be a home for us at last, thank God! And it is only moving from one house to another, when we breathe our last. "I go to my Father." Then we have somebody who knows us there. Yes, we have a parent in heaven watching us, guiding us, and waiting for us.

"He that believeth in me shall never die." Well, we shall find in heaven, then, abundant life; and decay will be unknown. "Where I am, there ye shall be also." We shall find Jesus in heaven; and we shall be with him, and we shall be one with him and with God.

And so in many and many a place throughout the New Testament can we gather glorious glimpses of the eternal world,— side lights, sketches, photographs, echoes, and knowledge enough to set the aching heart at peace, if we only rest on the mighty promises of God.

And how little we know about life, time, ourselves, or anything whatsoever! Life, forever a mystery, from the very moment that the babe cries out in fear as he greets the new world to the hour when the aged saint, with a smile on the face and a glory in the eye, takes the last breath and goes upward. How little we know about the earth journey; how short our sight, how imperfect our insight, how foolish our steps; what a labyrinth all the time; and how we stumble as we go along, fumbling in the dark continually, beset by trials, pains, sickness, seeming death, and being all the time seemingly alone! No, not alone: God is with us, Christ is at our side, the Holy Spirit encompasses our steps, there is a light in the window of heaven. And, if we know but little, that little is yet a good deal; for, if we try to do our best, we know at least that all heaven is on our side. And, although we cannot define life, nor explain it, nor fully manage it, nor in any way understand it, yet we can ask triumphantly, "If God be for us, who can be against us?" And we can be sure that, if we are on God's side, in the end the victory will be ours.

Time, too,— so swift!— how little we can explain it! To-day we are infants, to-morrow youths, next day in mid-life; and before we know it, and as we look back, it seems like the twinkling of an eye, we are in old age. And our birth has hardly been proclaimed, when it is announced that we are no more upon the earth, and in heaven, it is said, a child is born. And yet, although time can be so little measured, the little measure that we can get of it is a great benediction. We at least can know that it belongs to Almighty God, that it is united to eternity, that it is a loan to us for a while, that we are responsible for the way in which we manage it, and yet, if we will, that we can fill it with holiness, cover it with peace, send it away with glorious gifts, and make it give a good report of our doings at the throne of Almighty God.

We cannot make time stop, but we can make it bless us while it lasts; and we can send it away in joy, peace, love, and holiness.

And how little we know of ourselves; how very little we can know of the wonders of the body, even although our anatomical skill be very great; how little can we know of the glories of the mind, however acute as metaphysicians we may be by all confessed; how little can we understand about the soul, although we try with all our powers to belong to God and Christ and to be crowned with the Spirit! And yet the little that we do know about the human frame leads us to adore the Infinite Wisdom that made us what we are; the small conception that we have of mental power makes us bow low before the Omniscience that granted to us such twinkling sparks of his almighty thoughts; and the faint acquaintance that we have of the capacity of the soul makes us reverence with peculiar awe the great Soul of souls, by whom all souls are quickened into everlasting life.

"How little a portion is heard of him!"

Well, we must admit that the direct information about Almighty God is small, very small; and also that that which is told is very hard to be fully understood. And yet the indirect knowledge of God is very great, as the echoes come to us through nature, revelation, events, and the human soul; and so, day by day, we gather up hints of his marvellous power, his rich knowledge, and his never-ceasing love,— sparks, it may be, when compared with the reality, but sparks that will at some time, in God's holy time, here or hereafter, kindle up a great conflagration of light, glory, splendor, love, and holiness.

Faber says, and with his words we will close: —

> "Workman of God! oh, lose not heart,
>   But learn what God is like;
> And in the darkest battle-field
>   Thou shalt know where to strike.
> Thrice blest is he to whom is given
>   The instinct that can tell
> That God is on the field when he
>   Is most invisible."

XIII.

TRUE CHRISTIANS.

"One fold, one shepherd." — ST. JOHN x. 16.

I HAVE taken these words just as they stand in the old translation of the New Testament, although in this discourse I shall endeavor to preserve the spirit of both the old and the new version. The statement that we find in these words of old is one that no one on the earth can possibly doubt; and it is the only sentence in the Holy Bible, probably, that has not been questioned, for education, prejudice, partisanship, and self-love will always sustain it, vote for it, almost worship it.

At birth we are introduced, directly or indirectly, into the belief that there is but one right course; and the most liberal fathers and the greatest bigots that have charge of a family teach the children substantially the same lesson as regards the one way, the one fold, and the one Shepherd. Sabbath-schools are founded that the lambs may be taught this glorious fact, while church catechizing, argument, and preaching aim to bring all minds to the same striking idea. Why, then, are there so many different ways of thinking, so many standards of the infallible faith, so many roads that are said to be the only way to heaven, so many folds that are each marked as special, and so many views of Christ that are all said to be true?

The why lodges among the mysteries of God, but the fact is so sadly true that we can none of us deny it.

The universal definition of the words that we have placed at the head of our discourse is "my fold": this is the correct one. I am right, and you, my neighbor, are wrong; and in the end, if you wish to be saved, you must agree with me, accept my views, and sign my creed. My views of the Redeemer are the sound conceptions that at last will meet the approbation, the acceptance, and the enthusiastic fellowship of all real disciples. Such assertions on each side and on every side are very earnest, striking, and eloquent, so that we cannot doubt that the speakers mean just what they say; for they always use emphatic language and clear English, which cannot be misconceived. Every person also takes pains to spread his views. Vessels are chartered, missionaries are ordained, wealth is expended, books are printed, and churches are built, — all that peculiar views of Christianity may be spread everywhere and at all seasons; and time, labor, and expense are accounted as nothing, provided the children of God can be evangelized in one stated way. All parties, too, are apt to claim peculiar immunities, special powers, and inherited graces, and seem to take it for granted that they have the right alone to be God's ambassadors for building up the church of to-day and the church of the future.

This very pretence, however, explodes itself in the utterance; for all such work is placed in the Redeemer's blessed hands, and every sect that tacitly admits the possession of it rebels against Heaven, and will suffer for so great and so heavy a claim.

What are the proofs that any one sect offers that it alone is right, and that all others are wrong? Is it on the ground of being in the majority? Why, then, those who worship idols are right; for they outnumber all others. Or, to come to Christianity, then the Roman Catholics are right; for they outnumber the Protestants. Taking this ground, we must be either pagans or Roman Catholics. Do we use the plea of antiquity? Then we must be Jews or servants of the pope; for back of Judaism no instituted religion can possibly go, and back of the Church of Rome no form of Christianity is able to trace its certain birth. Shall our plea be that the holy Bible indorses our claims? But here we notice a sharp conflict between equally mighty minds and equally pious spirits, who assert clashing doctrines and call upon the Bible as a witness.

We are surely thrown from our track by maintaining a position like this, when it is very evident that mighty holiness and powerful reason in blessed coalition are all the time combating enemies of the same stamp. I admire Thomas à Kempis, the Catholic; and so also I love Luther, the Protestant. Yet both read their Scriptures very differently.

The characters of both Servetus and Calvin are to

be respected, yet these two were not the best of friends. Pascal and Whately were men of giant minds, yet not of the same church. So I might enumerate till my breath should cease the names of good, great, and holy men who differed in their interpretations of the Divine Record.

Some may say, however, We know that we are right, and there is no need of any discussion. But are we to trust in holy things to limited human knowledge or to Divine Proclamation? If to human knowledge, what special person shall we select as an expositor; and, if to the Divine Proclamation, are not all of us at liberty to judge of that?

We must either give up our Protestant faith or else we must allow every child of God perfect freedom of thought and expression.

We are hypocritical Protestants the very moment that we become bigoted; and, if we find ourselves outside of the region of a religious charity, in order to be honest we ought to join the "Mother Church."

Rome notices strictly our quarrels and our denials to each other of Christian privileges and of the Christian name; and she feeds herself upon the thought that eventually, when we are sick of our false freedom, we shall be glad to be encircled in her loving arms.

Where, then, can the one fold and the one shepherd be found? and where shall we look for the true Church of God?

Among all denominations where there is one true

spirit and one spiritual life. God is a spirit, and God is life. He takes sides with no one party: he is the Universal Father. He looks not at our lips, but upon our hearts; and he is to be worshipped, not by ritual alone, not by mysticism alone, and not only by articles of confession, however elaborated in writing, but only is he to be reverenced in spirit and in truth. He cares nothing for the badge on the forehead, whether there be engraved Unitarian or Baptist, Orthodox, Episcopalian, Methodist, Universalist, or Roman Catholic; but he asks for the badge on the heart, whether there be written "Holiness to the Lord," "All that I have is thine," "Thy will be done," and whether there Jesus has placed his peculiar mark, and whether there the Holy Spirit beautifully rests.

After all, my dear friends, there is but one rallying point, the cross, and one leader, the Lord Jesus Christ. Just here, brother, sister, whatever your name, we can stand together, holding each other by the hand, lifting our eyes heavenward, and asking unitedly, with fervor, unction, and an abiding love, that our lives may be somewhat in accordance with the "Pattern" that is set before us in the Mount.

Thus the true ones in all churches can be one in nature, purpose, affection, and hope, having one "Anchor" and looking to one common home as a blessed haven for the weary and penitent soul throughout eternal ages. I never did believe in being too particular about special names; and in the churches that God has given to me those of all denominations have gathered together with God as Father, Jesus as Lord, and the Holy Spirit as Comforter, and, under such an inspiration, all have hoped to march toward the gate of the Holy City with the banner of a perfect unity held serenely and trustingly before the eyes of all the inhabitants of earth and heaven. May such a spirit dwell with us now, and abide with all people everywhere! The new religion — final, perfect, pure — was that of Christ and love. His great command, his all-sufficing precept,— was it not love? So says Bailey, the Universalist. Hear also the Trinitarian Archbishop Wake's words,— "Who would not wish to see those days when, a general reformation, a true zeal, and a perfect charity passing through the world, we should all be united in the same faith, the same worship, the same communion and fellowship one with another?"

A Methodist brother remarks that, since the day of our Lord's personal ministry, his disciples have altered the shibboleth of Christianity,— that the test question is not now, "Simon Peter, lovest thou me?" but, "Simon Peter, thinkest thou as I do?" From all parts of the Church we have loud dissents to the sectarian spirit; and we perceive a restless desire that party bonds may be broken, and that true worth may be published, under whatever ecclesiastical garments it may be concealed.

The real Church is composed of such men as Bailey, Wake, Whitefield, Campbell, Comings, Parr,

Chalmers, Taylor, Stuart, Bond, James, Magoon, Channing, King, Ballou, Brooks, and millions of others who do not rest content with technicalities, but who love God, however manifested, cling to Jesus, however described, adore the Holy Ghost, whether a personality or a spirit, and who work for the mental and the spiritual culture of man, wherever he is found. The proselyting spirit, if conducted by bigotry, is the spirit of antichrist; and there is no truth that is so palpable as that. If I should attempt to encircle a man with my definitions and to bind him to them alone, I mislead him, I make myself the Christ, and I deny the Lord; for my statements concerning divine truth, and your statements, unless we both are divine, contain a great deal of error.

We have no right to say to any human being, Here is the Bible, and in it recline only such and such truths as we now describe; and, unless you believe those truths, you are certainly lost. But we should say to all, Here is the Bible, and in it abide truths which, if obeyed, will save the soul; and now search for yourselves what those truths are.

You all remember, perhaps, that Charles IV., after his abdication, amused himself by trying to make a number of watches go exactly together. But, constantly foiled in his attempt, he exclaimed, "What a fool I have been to neglect my own concerns and waste my whole life in a vain attempt to make all men think alike on matters of religion, when I cannot even make a few watches keep time together!"

The Gospels are full of expositions of their own liberality.

We read that those who were detected by the disciples in the casting out of evil spirits with the name of Jesus on their lips and with his love in their hearts, although not directly inaugurated into the number of those who followed Jesus, and although reprimanded by the apostles, were acknowledged and commended and received by the Master.

We find, as we turn over the pages of the Book of Acts, that those were accounted believers who had never even heard of the Holy Ghost, although afterward their ignorance was dispelled by special instruction.

We have heard of the terrible rebuke which the Pharisees received who compassed sea and land that they might gain one convert.

The moment any body of men, in any sect, claim to be alone in the right, and denounce all others as wrong, that moment these separatists become Pharisees as the Hebrew name betokens, and that moment the frown of the Lord rests upon them. There is but little difference between the Pharisees of Jerusalem and those of New England at this hour; for they partake of the same qualities of character, and they are found in greater or less numbers in every sect, village, and city, and they abide everywhere.

The preacher is not to point out the persons who are thus Pharisaical, else he himself would err; but the conscience of each one of us must answer guilty or not guilty at the bar of Almighty God. What, then, are the true tests by which we can each of us ascertain whether we belong to the one great fold and whether we are following the one true shepherd? Is our faith all the time blossoming and blooming into charity?

While we believe a certain set of truths clearly, earnestly, and without the shadow of a doubt, do we really love those who think very differently, who treat our most cherished visions with scorn, and who deem that we are standing on a very unsafe foundation?

Do we pray for our opponents in all sincerity, trusting that they, in time, may be led into that very road which we conceive to be the sure one, or that they may, by some blessed interposition of Almighty God, be uplifted to glory by their own course? Do we believe that heaven has mansions large enough for all phases of disciples, and are we willing that every Christian, under whatever banner he may rally, should be gathered into the great kingdom of the saints? If we can give an affirmative answer to all these searching questions, we are of the true church, and we are enfolded in the tender, gracious, and beautiful recognition of the good Shepherd. But we are not of the true church, God says and Jesus and the Holy Spirit declare, no matter what name we take, if we become critical, cynical, and selfish, and more anxious to manage souls than to leave the management to Almighty God.

We are not true Christians if we delight in an

opponent's failure; if we employ wicked stratagems in order to insure success to our cause and to extend our influence; if we speak ill, privately or upon the housetops, of other churches; if we are saddened at the success of rivals; and if we enjoy the thought that we are to be saved and that all others are to be lost.

We would not, by these remarks, discourage any of the earnest efforts of any denomination that are exerted for the upbuilding of influence and for the increase of disciples; but let only such efforts that claim to be in behalf of Christianity be conducted in a Christian spirit, for temper is sometimes mistaken for religion, and false zeal often works under the prestige of the cross.

The murder of the Huguenots in France is a sad comment upon perverted religious efforts.

When Mary, Queen of Scots, was put to death, history recorded the terrible fact that enthusiasm is something different from Christianity, that rancor can enter queenly and sacerdotal hearts, and that envy may easily apologize for its outbursts under the convenient guise of love for the Church.

When those called Quakers in New England were driven hither and thither, placed in the stocks, scourged and imprisoned, and put to death, the sad wails that ascended from the lips of those meek sufferers, piercing with solemnity the centuries, attest that bigotry is a sin, and that persecution is never persuasion, and that it always kills out the spiritual life of the persecutors. Freedom must be given to all, or else all are slaves; and the moment that a line is drawn, that moment the spirit of liberty is crushed.

God has set before all his children certain truths; but he leaves the reception of them, the definition of them, and the application of them to each one of us. And we each one are to answer, not to each other, but to him; and we each are to judge, not each other, but ourselves.

"One fold, one shepherd." My friends, unless we establish ourselves upon this broad platform, we shall always be in the dark, and frequently be upset; but, with Jesus for our Leader, with all Christians for our friends, with God as our Father, and with heaven for our home, we are safe, we have found the true church, and we shall gain at last everlasting peace.

"One fold, one shepherd." John Taylor says, and with his words we will close: —

> "As the good Shepherd leads his sheep
>   Through paths secure,
> And while afold by night they sleep
>   Doth keep them sure,
> So the 'True Shepherd,' Christ, our souls doth guide,
> Safe in his eye, protected by his side.
>
> "Great Shepherd! do we know thy voice
>   And follow thee?
> Is thy safe fold our rule and choice
>   From bondage free?
> Upheld by faith, the obedient sheep shall stand,
> And none shall pluck them from my Father's hand.

"Shepherd, with joy we hear thy call
  That leads to heaven.
Let none from that salvation fall
  So freely given;
But, as thy sacred records long foretold,
Be the wide-peopled earth one happy fold."

XIV.

THE EXCLUSIVE SPIRIT.

"No room for them in the inn." — ST. LUKE ii. 7.

I AM inclined to think that there would have been room for them in the inn on that first Christmas Day, spare chambers somewhere; nay, more, all the best houses in the place, if only they had been dressed a little more splendidly, had possessed great names, and had been high priests, or Roman governors, or those well known to have large means. But they were looked upon as only a man and a woman from Bethlehem or Nazareth who applied; ones not very high up according to the scale of mere human measurement,— and therefore, of course, on the world side there was no room for them in the inn.

When we apply at a public house for accommodations, it makes all the difference in the world what we are, or what we are thought to be, or what we seem to be, or what we pretend to be, whether we are treated kindly or roughly; and this ought not so to be, yet it always has been and it will be so for some time yet, until we are thoroughly possessed of the Christian spirit and are really willing to live up to what we preach. Certainly, if that landlord of old could have looked into futurity, could have sifted coming days, and could have known what you and I know, every room in the inn would have been at the command of the applicants, and nothing for which they asked would have been kept back.

I have taken this little incident of a past age that we may gain, on this holy Christmas Sabbath, some lessons from it; that we may learn not to be too exclusive, not to judge from appearances, and not to weigh any one too hastily. Some of us read characters better than others; but all of us are more or less dazzled by pretence, judge too hastily from very slight grounds, and are carried away by our fancies.

Look first on the bad side. There is apt to be no room in many places for the modest man or woman; and those who will not push themselves into notice are very apt to be kept in the background, so that, really, very often, some very splendid people are working out of sight, are standing in entirely too low a sphere, and are throwing their fragrance away in a small circle, while really humanity aches for their presence, power, and influence. Yet, giants as they are, they stand back, are content with being unnoticed and unknown, and are diamonds concealed, buried, flashing in the dark. And so much is this the case that some wits have said that the best preparation for a lofty station was mediocrity. There is no room in a great many places for the honest man or woman. I am sorry to say that real, genuine honesty is at a tremendous discount, and that we cannot to-day deal with each other thoroughly on the square without creating considerable of a noise; for fashion, speculation, and notoriety have so sent their fangs into the heart, manners, and habits of the people that it is very hard work to find anybody who never in any way turns aside from the truly straight line.

"Tell me," said one of my good friends, who came as near being perfect as perhaps any one in the flesh could, "tell me my faults." Yet, good as he was, had I been able to have picked out any weakness,— that perhaps only made his virtues more resplendent from the contrast,— had I picked them out and said, In just such a place you are weak, lacking, deficient, I know a flush would have come to his cheek, a deeper glow to his heart, and an impatient fire to his eye, while our intimacy would have received a blow that it would have taken an eternity to cure. I cannot tell why it is. I know it ought not so to be, and I am sorry that personal pride is so great; yet all of us recoil more or less from the plain-dealing person having but very little place for him or for her inside of our hearts. In some quarters there is but little room for the strictly and thoroughly Christian man or woman. We all differ so much in our likes and dislikes, in our impressions and convictions, in our way of looking at the same thing or of speaking of the same object, that in some families, or in some stores, or in many assemblies, the real and solid Christian is out of place. How many dear, good souls,— devout, aspiring, earnest, loving, and holy,— in the sacred circle of the family, dare not tell what they think, or look what they feel, or hardly act as they desire, because so many under the same roof would misunderstand the exhibition, or ridicule the conviction, or entirely repudiate the reality!

A wife may cling to the altar, while the husband clings only to mammon; a husband may clasp the cross, while the wife clasps only the world; a daughter may look to heaven, while both parents worship only pleasure; or brothers and sisters may be as far apart from all sympathy as the North from the South Pole. And there sometimes seems to be no possible chance for a good, clear, glorious outpouring of the soul till the angel of death comes, making that formerly seemingly frivolous home a cathedral, revealing the saints that had so long been masked, opening fresh avenues of conviction, conversion, and splendor to the thoughtless ones, and re-creating, as it were, those who before had been so icy, severe, and friendless. I am not so opposed to the "confessional" as many, could it only be rightly conducted, could it only be placed beyond the tarnish of the slightest sneer, and could the faintest breach of clerical confidence be punished severely as the most terrible crime; for then I think, with such a means for the unburdening of the human heart, the regeneration of the world would the more speedily follow, the kingdom of Christ be the more surely set up, and broken hearts get a comfortable healing. But now we dare not speak to anybody, we dare not tell anybody, and we are worn down and out by keeping our own secrets; and so we brood, worry, agonize, and feel lonely, sad, deserted. We know God is near and Jesus precious, but we want something more; we want something human; we want the pressure of a hand, the glance of an eye,—one pitying, consoling, elevating, and redeeming word. But, ah! generally, society has no place where the Christian, or the one who wants to be a Christian, or anybody in trouble or despair or darkness, can go for light, peace, and joy. Let us look now on the good side.

There really is no true room in this world for anybody but the modest ones; for the question is not, Who have the prizes? but, Who move time and eternity, who shake earth and heaven, who finally conquer souls? I tell you the prairie rose is not really wasted. No, although no human eye has ever seen it, no human hands ever plucked it, no graceful parlor been consecrated by its beauty; and I do not believe that God ever put diamond souls in the world only to shine in a dark place, useless, forlorn, and utterly neglected.

The modest ones do have their say, although they seem not to speak; they do uplift humanity, although they seem not to move; and, like electricity, they permeate and inspire the atmosphere in which they move. You cannot always tell where, how, when, and how much; yet the power is all around, upheaving sin, banishing weakness, and establishing rectitude.

The pygmies, however highly perched, really

accomplish nothing: they are simply excrescences. They stand on the throne, to be sure; but that is all. But the power is behind the throne, and the kings often are those uncrowned.

I wish I could gather all the really modest ones in the world together in some one church, and I am not sure that the building would have to be very large even then. I would say to them: You think that you are nothing, but really you are all in all. You seemingly occupy the smallest stations, yet I tell you really you are reigning on thrones of gold, while all around your brows are the sparkling jewels of heaven.

You sometimes think your life a failure; but I tell you it is not, unless light be a failure, air a mistake, breath useless. For I label you as the light, air, breath of humanity, since, without your aid, love, blessing, and silent but potent quickening, all would perish. Do not despond; for your names are written very bright, beautifully large, and gloriously clear in God's list of saints, so that you will some day rejoice in a happy coronation, being placed high up among the royal ones of the Celestial City.

Again, the honest men or women are the only ones that can be truly happy or useful in this world, the only ones really for whom room should be made.

It is not, perhaps, necessary to tell all that we think; but it is necessary that all we do tell should be just what we do think, with all varnish, sweetening, and frescoing left off. Those of us who prevaricate or misstate or tell falsehoods, because it is the fashion, have really no right to be in a globe where nature never utters a falsehood, where all the oracles of God are true and sure, and where everything in the heavens above, or in the earth beneath, or in the waters under the earth, is so exact. Certainly, dishonest ones are out of tune, out of place, and thoroughly disordered, where all the laws of nature and of nature's God are so punctual, persistent, and unvarying. Advance, ye honest ones, and claim the heritage of space with which you are in such sacred harmony. Raise up your flag of honor, with its appropriate and grand symbol of righteousness, and never let it get soiled or twisted or abused; and stand by your colors, no matter how many ridicule or injure or try to upset you. Stand by your colors, and then God will stand by you. The good Shepherd will take your hand, leading you into all pleasant and peaceful paths; and the angels will cluster around you in a glorious company, wreathing your brows with spiritual garlands, and shouting, too, their hosannas unto heaven that in the great battles of life a few have been found faithful and true. At once take possession of the land; for it is yours by right of gift, by right of inspiration, by right of conquest, and by the inherent right of your unsullied, glorious, and beautiful integrity. There really is in this earth no place for any one but the Christian man and the Christian woman. A great many not deserving such a name are occupying the land; but they are usurpers, so that some day there must be an awful reckoning for them to meet. I believe firmly in a millennium. I know not when; yet it will come, when the world will be given to those that really own it,—namely, the disciples of our Lord and Saviour Jesus Christ.

But, really, now only such disciples get the good of life; for only such as they know what real joy, solid peace, and perfect gain are, and they alone can make every day an anthem, every event but a string in the harp on which the choicest spiritual music is played, every joy a sparkling gem, every pain equally bright, and all things like a mosaic richly tessellated by angel fingers and worthy the admiration of the saints.

Only the Christian can face disaster with a smile, grasp the crown of thorns with no recoil, change tears into pearls, and make heaven everywhere.

"No room in the inn."

But, my brother, my sister, have you any room in your soul for faith, hope, love, and all righteousness? Let us each one put this great question to our souls this glorious Christmas week. Are we prepared to receive God's messengers, are we in so good attune with Heaven that we are sure of making the most of this lower life and of receiving a solid title-deed to all the pleasures and profits that it can possibly yield?

We all want not only room for us in heaven, but room for us here; for we do not wish to be out of harmony even here, and we want to get the most out of each day and each hour in the flesh, and we are not satisfied with picking up pins as we walk along, for we want to pick up spiritual gold. And, however successful we may be in material gains, we crave something better, something purer, and something holier; but we shall never possess what we need, nor stand where we should, nor become anything like what God means us to be, till we give ourselves up to the gracious keeping of the good Shepherd, and until Jesus Christ is born in our hearts.

There is no life for the soul, no inn for the heart, and no peace in time and in eternity, without the blessed inspiration of the Holy Ghost, that is conveyed to earnest believers through the unceasing tenderness, ever-watchful love, and constant benediction of both Father and Son.

May we each say in borrowed words: —

> "I am thine, O Lord, I have heard thy voice,
> And it told thy love to me;
> But I long to rise in the arms of faith,
> And be closer drawn to thee.
> Draw me nearer, nearer, blessed Lord,
> To the cross where thou hast died,
> Draw me nearer, nearer, blessed Lord,
> To thy precious bleeding side.
>
> "Consecrate me now to thy service, Lord,
> By the power of grace divine.
> Let my soul look up with a steadfast hope,
> And my will be lost in thine."

XV.

THE GLORY OF NAZARETH.

"Can there be any good thing come out of Nazareth?"—St. John i. 46.

I AM not surprised that such a question was asked, for there is something about its whole texture that is extremely natural. Nazareth was an inconsiderable place, has been so ever since, and will probably continue to be so for many years to come; and it hardly seemed possible then, as it would hardly seem possible now, that it could be the home of anybody very great and holy. And yet, if we will only look into the philosophy of events a little more curiously, and run our eyes and souls down the centuries, and place in a line by themselves all the mighty personages of history, we shall be utterly surprised to see that a majority of the leading persons in the world took their start from the most obscure spots, so that, if a rule were to be formed as to the needed conditions for the establishment of a great character, fact would force us to say, while inclination would urge us to deny, that his or her birth, or his or her education, must be in a town or in a city of little or of no reputation. Again, we should be apt to say that mighty events must have a tremendous cause; that no city could be built up nor overthrown, no government established nor demolished, no principle be inaugurated, and nothing grand get supremacy, save by a fearful upheaving or by an awful explosion at the very beginning.

Still, if we will place the mammoth events of history in a row by themselves and conscientiously sift out their embryonic life, we shall be surprised to detect the tiny mustard-seeds that were the parents of such wonderful disclosures. But, despite evidence and notwithstanding sight and insight, we keep exclaiming, "Can there be any good thing come out of Nazareth?" The truth is, we none of us really know what is great or little, while every day we get things terribly transposed as we attempt to define them by our spiritual and mental dictionary. Our prejudices run away with our judgment, and the outside of an event takes captive the imagination, while we have no desire and no heart to penetrate to its substance, — even to the very core of reality. So that thunder seems more potent to us than the silent rays of the sun, and the flash of lightning more terrible and destructive than noxious air.

Let us look a little closely at this matter.

A great many things are viewed as Nazareth now, and are treated with contempt. So we are apt to call all that do not agree with our opinions, do not move in our circle, — all that we do not understand and all that a majority of people have united to condemn. People constantly get together in classes, setting up certain opinions as infallible, and reading out of sense, good fellowship, and recognition every one who dares to set up an opposition. So every State is filled up with parties who each frown on the other, and esteem as worthy of notice only those carrying their badge; and everything else is Nazarene,— not to be allowed, not to be recognized, and not to be complimented for a moment. Ay, some go so far as to say that that one is not honest who does not stand on their platform. I believe, free as we are in the United States of America, that there is no place in the world where the despotism of opinion rages with such savage violence. Some people allow, it is true, all to think as they please; but, if any happen to think as they do not please, they soon give them to understand that they shall in the future avoid their company.

"You may vote for whom you like," said the chief officer in Napoleon's army: "every one must exercise a free and an unimpeded course, and no one will be influenced in the least; but," he added in a whisper, "those who do not vote for Napoleon will be shot." Of course, the result was a spontaneous, unanimous, and a wonderful victory for the emperor.

Now, friends, we do not practise shooting in such cases, it is true; but a great many people go as far as the law will let them go, wishing all the time that they could give harder blows.

Why, can any one be good for anything who sees truth differently from what we do?

This is the seething question all the time in the centre of some minds, which perhaps few would like to confess. Ah! we have learned a great deal when we each are enabled to say, I may be wrong. Again, there are some people who do not have a sufficient charity for those who belong to what are falsely called the lower ranks of society.

Can any good possibly come from what are called the obscure places of the world?

That is the unkind speech of some of those who call themselves the favored children of God.

They sometimes dream that privileges are guaranteed only to a certain elect company; and yet all the time is this false idea exploded by some stalwart soul who steps from the lowest depths with majestic tread, sweeping all opposition into blessed oblivion and making even granite walls crumble to dust at his touch.

See there in the woods a little homely boy, overgrown, ragged, and splitting rails with all his might and main, that he may get a little bread for his mouth and more clothing for his limbs. He, of course, you say, will come to nothing,— no more than the packhorse in the mill, who treads his weary round till death. So you turn away, you proud one, with a sneer; and you go the other side, you privileged one, laughing at the oddity of the lad. Yet let one lift the vail of history, and there will be seen one of the most distinguished men of America; a man whose name rings around the world as a hero and a martyr;

a man who trampled all classes under his feet, rushed to the topmost round of the social ladder, and passed suddenly from sight at the acme of his fame. And of another one might we speak, honored all over the country during life for integrity, ability, courage, and holiness; a man of principle and a man of prayer; Chief Justice, and chief in justice, honor, truth, and righteousness, one who seemed in early youth terribly put back by the death of his father when he was only twelve years old, yet who stepped in front of all difficulties, and kept rising and rising, from student, school-teacher, lawyer, author, councilman, senator, governor, Secretary of the Treasury, candidate for the Presidency, and finally occupant of that majestic position in law which he filled so faithfully and powerfully almost up to the very minute that his soul passed through the gate of heaven.

So with thousands of others that I might name, who have not waited for your smile nor for my approbation, nor for anybody's favor, but have taken opportunity with a wrenching hand, a stubborn will, and have caught golden prizes from its tight and holy embrace.

Again, those we do not understand we are apt to think as not worth much. They may take as high a position or a higher one than we do; but, if we do not understand them, we think they ought to be consigned to oblivion,— as if our poor thought were to be the only measurement of all right and all righteousness.

I have never yet been able to see what makes so many people think so much of themselves, intellectually, morally, and spiritually. The best people, and the brightest, are those who are the most humble and the least forth-putting; while it seems as if those of the false stamp tried to make up in mere foam what they lack in solid weight. Because I cannot comprehend you, or because you cannot comprehend me, is no valid proof that either of us can be called foolish; and he alone is the witless one who dares to call the other a hard and a wicked name.

Once more, a large number hold it as an established rule that everything is to be condemned that the majority of the people in the world condemn.

This in a great many cases is very safe reasoning; but it does not hold good invariably, else Jesus of Nazareth must be wiped out of history immediately at his birth, and all Christianity now must be expunged, while Paganism takes its place. In great crises of natural life or of the world's experience it is the minority who generally have the best of it, as you will readily see as you scan patriarchal records, Hebrew tribes, Christianity through all its vicissitudes, and the landing of the Pilgrim Fathers so many years ago. Protestantism itself is yet in the minority. Then, really, it is a very dangerous work for a majority, however noble, to throw sarcasm upon a minority, however dejected and forlorn. I am glad, for one, and I think it was a grand thing, that Jesus did come from both Bethlehem and Nazareth; for thus we were taught that worth makes the place, and that no place of itself can really confer honor or shame. I do not care where anybody is born, but I do want to know how people live and what characters they carry into the eternal kingdom.

I want to know how they have raised themselves up, despite adverse circumstances, and how they have forced a reluctant world to bow to their great honors. Are you the son of a king? Well, you are no better for that,— nay, I fear that you are to be pitied; for a great many king's sons have done nothing but run down hill all through life.

Are you the child of a peasant? Then you are none the worse for that,— nay, I think your future must be very brilliant if you will only be faithful to your opportunities; for many of our Alpine men have started from localities that gave no pledge for future splendor.

Nobody expected that any good would come out of Nazareth. It was altogether too obscure a place. It was not worth a random thought. The scholar and the aristocrat would have preferred Jerusalem for the coming deliverer. Not so thought Almighty God, and not so does he deal with the children of men. He shows the emptiness of mere opinion, the folly of a starched aristocracy, the narrow limits of pretended scholarship, and the weakness of a bigoted superstition, by making the great epoch of the ages culminate in Bethlehem and Nazareth. Never was such a grand blow given to the ideas of the mere people of the world as when the Son of God was born in a place where least of all the great and the noble wished to find him.

Yet do we think enough of this mighty fact? Are the people of to-day any more wise than those of old? What is it now that really commands our deepest admiration?

I speak to those who call themselves Christians, to those who believe in Jesus, and to those who feel that they are really the consecrated children of Almighty God. What dazzles now the most, worth or show, the golden character or gold in the purse, the nobleman on the throne or the nobleman in rags? Have we not all at this time a prejudice against our Nazareth, feeling its decided inferiority and the impossibility that it shall ever be noted for anything whatever? Just so far as we give way to our prejudices, and just so far as we are overcome by the mere tinsel of life, and just so far as we blind ourselves against ragged worth and obscure splendor, so far are we like those of ancient days speaking in contempt of the grandest gifts of Almighty God.

"Can there be any good thing come out of Nazareth?" Yes, there can be good in Nazareth; and there has been, and there will be, good things coming out of just such places all the time. For the dear Father of us all is not tied down to human whim; and where he will he plants his jewels, so that in the darkest and in the deepest places some of the most magnificent specimens of his gracious benevolence can be daily found. Only let us keep our eyes, ears, and hearts open, and we shall be surprised how everywhere glory can come, and on all sides beauty spring forth, if we only so will. Oh, what good has come out of Nazareth, and how the force there created has upheaved the world, and how that little place now engirdles in its divine references all the mightiest enterprises of time and all the glorious epochs of eternity! So will it ever be.

Glory be to Almighty God for the triumphs of the babe in Bethlehem and the grand history of the young life at Nazareth!

Glory be to his mighty name, that, contrary to all human opinion, in the face of prejudice, rank, and power, despite the proud Pharisee, the sceptical Sadducee, the seclusive Essene, the powerful Roman, the polished Grecian, and the fickle crowd, despite all philosophy and all poor mortal guessing, out of two little towns, sparsely settled and not much known, and of inhabitants generally rude and unrefined, there was born and there was educated one both divine and human, our Master and our Lord, by whose simple and majestic voice, by whose sacred and splendid teachings, by whose pure and holy character, there came forth a power which nearly nineteen centuries have not been able to crush, and before which idolatry and superstition and all sin have rushed into silence and fallen into shame!

Thanks be to the Father that he has thus taught all his children the true nobility of every mortal that breathes the breath of life, the rich possibilities, the gorgeous splendors, and the august coronations that hover over the brow of every babe, and the strange but beautiful mysteries that cling to his ever gracious guidance! Oh, let us rejoice that, in the unknown future that stands before us all, our destiny is not to be shaped by any poor arithmetic of any mortal prophecy, by any heavy clouds that in the beginning of our enterprises may seem to obstruct the way, and by any seeming disasters and apparent failures and wilful rebuffs. No, no! But all these coming years are to bring their gracious revelations or their more sombre benedictions, as they have been created or shaped or sanctified or redeemed by a wisdom that never errs, a power that never falters, a love that never cools, and a care always sweet and sublime.

Thus our future is beyond a peradventure, if we keep within the enclosure of a Christian obedience and by the rich valleys of a celestial devotion.

Think of these great realities, all ye who watch the unknown future, joyful or anxious, hopeful or sad, with a light in the eye or shadows on the brow; for, as you are held up by the almighty arm that can never falter, attended by the good Master's companionship that never forsakes the earnest disciple, girdled by the sacred soothings and the gracious inspirations of the Holy Spirit, and flanked so beautifully and so triumphantly by whole legions of angels, every day shall fall into a victory, every hour bring its gift, and the apocalypse of eternity be but one continued revelation of benediction and peace. So may it be with each and all of us, now and forever!

CHRISTMAS POEM.

Hark, the Christmas bells are ringing,
And the angel choirs are singing
   That Christ is born.
And wrong is conquered by the right,
A world is lifted into light,
   No more forlorn.

All the earth was sad and dreary,
And the human heart was weary,
   Till Christ did come.
And then the darkness fled away,
And holy love began its sway
   O'er hearth and home.

All glory be to God on high,
Let every mortal gladly cry,
   That Christ was given!
May Christ grant all the power to see,
As at his name they bend the knee,
   The way to heaven.

XVI.

THE WEDDING GARMENT.

"Friend, how camest thou in hither, not having a wedding garment?"
ST. MATT. xxii. 12.

THERE is a beautiful fitness, a musical chant, and inspiriting echoes in all God's works, ways, and promises. The garniture of the earth, however varied; the clothing of the heavens, however colored; and the constant wonders of nature,— all agree with the general design and harmonize with each other: there is no jar, nor discord, nor jostle; and the tones are charmingly sweet, in full accord, and with reconciling power, so that from the wide sweep of infinite space arises an anthem of delight, as a grateful response for the perfect, glorious, and striking fellowship. A comet is not a freak of nature, but a result of law; a volcanic eruption is not an insubordination against authority, but only the developing of a central order and the working out of the divine will; and everything is appropriate in God's creation, while this fact constitutes the grandeur of this great world that God has given to the children of men. The little wild flower that nestles in the forest has its part to play, its place to fill, and its influence to exert, just as well as the planets and the sun; and the insect that crawls at our feet has its work to do quite as clearly as the lion or the camel or the tiger, who seem made for a purpose more striking, attractive, and startling. In this world nothing is so insignificant as to be detached from the general service, nothing is so small as to be unnoticed by God, and nothing is so worthless as to be worthy of abuse; and so, on the other hand, nothing is so grand as to stand aloof from companionship, to attempt an independent career, and to hold in contempt all lesser powers. No: in God's world everything is important, has its work to do, and all things have a grandeur of their own, be it leaf or be it star, be it the ocean or be it a dewdrop, be it man or be it an angel. We discover also, if we study nature deeply, cheerfully, and religiously, that each of nature's children is prepared to work, is attired for the occasion, and has the wedding garment that is especially needed for the glorious service.

The seasons all march along dressed as they should be,— spring with its buds, summer with its flowers, autumn with its fruits, and winter with its snow; and they all shake hands together in a glorious, a splendid, and an unbroken fellowship. Spring says, I will unlock the frosty ground that winter has starched and chilled, I will tap the trees and make them show their richness, I will start the waters from their icy slumbers, and I will call to activity a sleeping world. Summer says, I will go farther than this: I will decorate the earth with beauty, fill it with fragrance, convert it into a paradise, and send a genial heat over all is inmates. And autumn says, I will ask for results, see what all this thawing, blooming, and blushing has accomplished, demand fruits, and give to the world a blessed harvest, as the spontaneous offerings of a liberated soil. Winter exclaims, I will put all nature to sleep, for the workers have worked long enough: I will cover the world with a shroud and touch it with a magic wand, so that all things shall rest awhile and find a glorious peace.

Ah! these seasons agree to do their part: each one gives way to the other, and they all appear in the garb that is most natural, fitting, and beautiful. So in all the doings of nature we discover the same benignant consistency. And should not the children of God copy this splendid law?

There is a place for us all: we all must be clothed for that place; and each one of us should take up the special field that is assigned for our culture.

There is a spring, a summer, an autumn, and a winter in the history of us all; and let them be met, acknowledged, improved, and glorified.

This fact in material matters is readily, gladly, and earnestly confessed.

The mechanic must be something of a mathematician, skilled with tools, have a genius for his work, and be clothed with the wonderful gift of inventive curiosity, or else he is a failure, a disgrace, and sinks into oblivion. The merchant must understand the principles of trade; the laws that invest sales and purchases, both at home and abroad; the habits, the customs, and the languages of the varied nations all over the globe; the tariff of the commodities that are found in different localities; and the right estimate of exchange. In fact, he must know all about all the thousand intricate regulations that adhere to a business career, or else he is a poor merchant, and will meet with but very little success. The professional man must be versed in letters, have a sound education, and the power of giving out thought, or else his profession will lose its dignity, beauty, and power. We all see this clearly enough; and so we build colleges, scientific schools, law schools, theological schools, medical schools, and endow with great liberality the professorships that are needed, striving to do all that we can, so that every man shall enter upon his work thoroughly prepared. This certainly is too evident to need a prolonged explanation.

If every "doctor" ought to have been a "minister," if every "minister" ought to have been a "merchant," if every "merchant" ought to have been a "mechanic," and if everybody be just where he ought not to be, into what a chaos the world would be thrown, and how quickly we should wish ourselves dead!

But, my dear friends, in the moral and in the spiritual character of all of us the law of appropriateness is also to be acknowledged, learned, and obeyed. We are all ordered to be good and to do good, each to a certain extent in a peculiar way; and, although now spiritual natures are so discordant, it is meant that they should be in a perfect, glorious, and benignant harmony.

I do not think that any of us can reach perfection here below, and I know that there is yet a great deal to be done by all of us before we come within sight of the mark which we ought to reach.

A man acquires a wonderful control of his temper, and then he thinks that he has reached to a very high standard of goodness; and so he has, but he has not secured everything, as he supposes, and there is much more for him to do. I am glad that he speaks kindly; but does he act kindly, thoughtfully, generously, and is he a man of prayer and principle? Is his heart gentle as well as his tones, and does he relinquish all his bad habits as well as his bad speech?

Again, a man is thoroughly honest; and then he thinks that honesty is enough. Well, it is a great virtue, in these days of temptation, to tell the truth, to act the truth, and to be full of integrity; but there is much more to be done, and many more virtues to be gained, before one becomes what he ought to be. For one must be devout as well as straightforward, gentle as well as exact, and pure as well as true.

So I might go on naming special virtues that we are apt to enthrone as great acquisitions, while we keep our eyes blind to our many deficiencies. Let each one who thinks that he is wearing a wedding garment examine himself closely and look to the very centre and circumference of his heart and life; for then it will be seen, I am sure, that there has been a false self-estimate. We may have the wedding gloves or the wedding vest, but we are not completely attired in the royal garb. One sad test of the great deficiency in the characters of the children of God is their lack of love for each other; and I am amazed at the perfect indifference many people exhibit about the welfare of others. For they live as if they had no concern with any one but their own families, as if all their duties and all their obligations rested at home. Here they are, surrounded by souls that are aching for light: here are their neighbors and their fellow-beings looking to them for counsel; but they wrap themselves up in their own self-sufficiency and say, "Who is my neighbor?" forgetting that everybody within reach is a neighbor, and not thinking that we are all ordained as ministers over God's parish, that is built everywhere and grows everlastingly. One of the articles of which the wedding garment is composed is humility; and, as long as we are satisfied with our abundance, or our good family, or our pre-eminent virtues, we shall be short of the material that is needed for the making of our spiritual attire.

I do not advise the breaking down of classes, for I suppose as long as the world exists there must be some kind of a social scale; but I do advise the breaking down of the aristocratic spirit, the utter extinction of Pharisaic exclusiveness, and the crushing of that jealous, ambitious, and Satanic temper that speaks, even when the voice is not used, to every less favored one, — "I am holier or better than thou."

The words of our text bid us always to be in a devout frame of mind; for there is no occasion, no company, and no possible moment, where it will do for us to put off our religion entirely.

So, most certainly, on every holy day that is set apart for worship, we should not forget the wedding garment. Have we all of us put that garment on to-day? Is our mind full of adoration, our heart full of peace, our soul full of God? And do we come here feeling ourselves weak? Are we seeking strength from the Father? Are we listening, not critically, but with a teachable spirit, being determined to go away better than we came; and do we always convert spiritual exercises into our deepest culture, so that, whenever we hear a prayer, or listen to a chant, or catch the faintest discourse upon God, goodness, and heaven, we are uplifted, inspired, and renewed?

It is no light thing that we gather together week after week for the worship of the Father and for the rededication of ourselves to his blessed service. And this Sunday worship should not merely be a form, should not congeal into a habit and be a fossil of the past; but it should blossom, blush, and ripen into a reality, — as real as life, as solemn as death, and as grand as eternity. The Sabbath Day is a spiritual feast that is spread by the Infinite One for the refreshment, the culture, and the salvation of his benighted children. And, no matter who the preacher may be,— strong or weak, eloquent or heavy, full of himself or full of God,— the day is the Lord's Day. And so also it is our day, and there are other voices than human pleading with our souls; while, if we be clothed in the right spirit, filled with the true thoughts, and if all through our natures the echoes of the Eternal be heard, then the "Lord's Day" will always be to us a delight, a benediction, and a peace.

But are there not too many everywhere that go to church to be entertained, to listen to grand music, to set a good example, and to pass away idle time, or for some purpose not in full accord with the divine will? Good music, earnest preaching, and neat and graceful attire are not to be despised; but they are far from indispensable, and we can do without them. For there can be a stirring cathedral service in each one's soul, although never a word be spoken. Although, like those called Quakers, our hour should be passed in meditation; and although in plainest dress we should sit upon rough boards,— even then we should be helped, if our hearts were true, tender, and right in the sight of God.

Ah! here is the secret: our hearts must be true, and then all things will fall into their proper place; and we shall look not mainly for the wisdom, work, and will of man, but for the voice, grace, and salvation of Almighty God.

It is a sad sign of the decline of religion at this day that people all over the world are seeking for something new, striking, and overwhelming all the time. They ask more for show than for substance, and look more for effect than reality. An intelligent man said to me not very long ago that, after all, what was needed in the pulpit was not so much a good sermon as a good voice, a fine manner, and an impressive delivery; and then he added,—no particular matter about the sermon! I am afraid that man does not always wear his wedding garment; but how many there are who are like him! Ah! where are we drifting, when we look for amusement, eloquence, and masquerade, and when we care so little for the simple gospel and its sublimest terms,—new birth, sanctification, salvation, redemption, Christ, and the cross? Ah! I fear we need to-day an awaking like that when Luther rent the Roman Catholic Church in twain, or when the Wesleys stirred the English Church to its centre. We need to take hold of sacred things with a live spirit; for the Bible must become to us a new book, dearer than ever before, truer than ever before, and not to be too lightly handled, too freely criticised, or too much let alone, but to be reverenced, obeyed, studied, and cherished, as containing the voice of Almighty God.

Let us all wake up from our comfortable slumbers, from our self-complacent habits, and from our listless manner, to a sense of the greatness of our make, the beauty of goodness, the majesty of the soul, and the glory of God. Let us wake up, so that we can enthrone religion in its right place as supreme ruler and guide,— no longer making it an attendant upon our whims, an embellishment of our characters, and in any way a second-rate concern. Let us wake up, till every thought shall be purified, every desire be cleansed, every word be holy, and every deed be true. Religion first, religion chief, and religion all in all, — above business, above pleasure, and above even life! Ah! this should be our motto day by day and hour by hour. Jesus Christ always wore the wedding garment, and he never forgot his high calling; and, place him where you would, he was always himself.

Whether he stood by priest or by peasant, before a crowd or in the sanctity of a home, on mountain top or in the centre of a lake, in the wilderness, tempted, or on the way to Jerusalem, glorified; transfigured on the mount or abased on the cross; speaking to Pilate in the judgment hall or giving his benediction to the watching disciples as he retreats to the heavens,— he is always himself, always ready for the occasion, and ever looks the right look, speaks the right word, and does the right thing.

It is a great relief to me, when I am wearied with the world's mistakes, oppressed by its weakness, and confounded by its follies, as I turn to my Master, and find One who never did anything out of the way, and who, under all provocations, never lost his self-command; who regulated his temper and his temperament so thoroughly after the divine law, and went through the world unspoiled by its temptations, unconquered by its trials, and undismayed by its abuses,— went through with the wedding garment never soiled, never torn, but always fresh, attractive, and beautiful, and always full of a splendor past description and a glory not of this world.

The wedding garment! That is the robe which you and I wish to wear, not only here, but when we enter heaven.

Certainly, we all of us have a great deal to do about this garment; for we all of us must soon pass away into the unseen.

The garment must be purchased, made up, worn; and it must be made richly, full of embroidery, covered with jewels, and magnificent and gorgeous.

But what is this garment? Why, it is our character,—our moral and our spiritual character: this is what we must enrich, enlarge, elevate, and spiritualize. Let us look to our temper: is it all that it should be,—sweet, serene, trusting, and devout? Let us look to our habits: are they methodical, charitable, and pure? Let us look to our hearts: are they loving, honest, earnest, and holy; and is the world better because we are living in it, and is God's kingdom advanced because we breathe the breath of life?

Can we find within our souls the temple of the Lord,—a temple so built as to encourage worship and work, while there is a place in it where the light of devotion never goes out?

Never let it be said of us that we are incomplete, out of place, wrongly clothed, careless of our privileges, and forgetful of our dignity. Never let this be said as long as we dwell in time or hope to live in eternity.

We are invited to the feast of God that is spread for us every day of our mortal and our immortal existence; and let us, then, prepare aright for its enjoyment, and wear the clothing so gloriously recommended by the apostle,— a clothing which can be obtained if we seriously ask, seek for, and demand it.

It is thus brilliantly described by Saint Paul: "The loins are to be girt about with truth, the breastplate is to be of righteousness, the feet are to be shod with the preparation of the gospel of peace, the shield is to be of faith, the helmet of salvation, the sword of the word of God."

Brothers and sisters, friends, children of God, disciples of Jesus, you who are soon to be angels, the garment is ready; and are you ready to wear it? Let each and all say Amen!

XVII.

THE OMNIPRESENCE OF THE ALMIGHTY.

"Not far from every one of us." — ACTS xvii. 27.

I SUPPOSE that every one of us, at certain times and in peculiar straits, either when the mind is troubled or the body is weak or the heart is sad; at times when self-sufficiency is seemingly buried forever out of sight,— at such times of overwhelming need, every one of us is oppressed with loneliness, helplessness, and wants comfort, aid, and strength, terribly craves the presence of somebody, a kindling eye, kindly face, an outstretched hand, a cordial word, a heart beating in union, affection, sympathy, encouragement, and benediction. For we all feel at such times that we cannot stand alone, and we cry out for the living God,— nay, for anybody living besides ourselves who can hold us up, keep our spirits up, give us faith, hope, pluck, nerve, and fresh power; and sometimes, for a while, we seem to be beating the air in vain.

There are times, too, of unconscious need, when we are none the less objects of pity, claimants for mercy, and utterly good for nothing unless lifted up, sustained, inspired, nourished, and glorified by some outside power. And so, in the hour of conscious and unconscious need, we hear — glory be to God through our Lord Jesus Christ! — the sublime, comforting, holy, and blessed announcement that the Almighty is not far from any one of us; that we are never left alone; that we are always watched, guided, preserved, and loved; and that we cannot slip away from the benignant gaze that forever looks down from above.

Have you ever seen a little child running away from his father, hiding behind tree or rock or house, and thinking it impossible that the place of retreat can be discovered, and yet the father sees the child all the time? And so God never loses sight of us, even when we run away, hide behind the tree of temptation, are covered by the rock of sin, and are seemingly sheltered in the house of rebellion. Even then God sees, watches, and knows.

So, too, the little child who runs away from his father is almost afraid all the time that he is hiding that father may not find him; that he will remain concealed forever; that there will be no more home, no more parents, no more brothers and sisters, — a grand desolation. And then, when the misery is overwhelming, father comes and takes his hand; and, oh, such a joy, such a laughing, and such inward peace! And so between us and God, if we run away from him, we begin, by and by, to feel that he may not find us, may leave us to ourselves, may never again take our hand; and, in our utter desolation, we find that he is close by us, saying, "My son or my daughter, give me thine heart." He is not far away from any one of us, — at our birth, in our temptations, in moments of great exigencies, when we are in terrible doubt which way to turn, when we travel away from home awhile, in sickness, in sorrow, in death, when we enter heaven, and all through eternity.

Probably there is no period in our existence when our helplessness is seemingly so great as when we are infants; for we can do nothing for ourselves then, and our food, clothing, and whole care depend on the kindness of somebody else, and our frail life, hanging upon a thread, rests upon the will of Almighty God.

It has been wisely ordered that the very helplessness of childhood should call out a corresponding pity, love, and protection from all within reach. So that any one who would abuse a little child is universally labelled as a monster; and the Italian Padrone in New York who maltreated so many little ones was severely punished, not only by the slow but sure process of law, but also by the quick scorn, censure, and indignation of all the fathers and mothers all over the land.

I think that one of the most glorious testimonies of the never-failing goodness of God is to be found in his constant watchfulness over the childhood of us all; and the human race would perish forever, were it not for this restraining hand.

What accidents the little ones escape, what providential rescues, what wonderful adventures, that, varied by one hair's breadth, would have proved terrible calamities! And cannot we all of us review our boyhood or girlhood and wonder at our escapes?—where, according to all the laws, we ought to have been burned or drowned or stabbed, and hurried out of existence. And yet we live, because the Infinite was not far from us: his hand tempered the blow, his love covered the disaster, his benediction averted death. And here we are, preserved, uplifted, sanctified, and safe, with proofs for a superintending Providence that no logic can drive from our breasts.

Again, he is not far from us in our temptations, the very time when we should perhaps suppose that he was absent or unconscious or careless about our welfare. What! by us in our temptations, and not drive the tempter away; not take away our inclination to be befooled; not consecrate our will, that it may restrain our lips, tie our hands, and make us safe? What! look on and see us reel, stagger, question, and almost yield? Can a Father do that?

Yes; and, if he did anything else, he would not be a wise Father. Does an earthly father allow a child to have no will, no judgment, no choice, no character, and bind the child to an iron necessity without the possibility of jostling his position one hair's breadth?

What is innocence worth, till it is made virtue by a personal resistance, until it has faced the foe and put him down, till it has seen the wrong and dismissed it, till it has fought the good fight and obtained the victory?

The Infinite Father is by when we are tempted; but he is all the time showing us the other side, giving us the power to balance the advantages of right and wrong, proving to us by our intuitions that there is a choice, and that, as we may make our choice, so shall we be consecrated or shamed.

He lets us be tempted, but he never gives us any temptation that we are not able to overpower if we desire; and, if we fall, it is our own fault: we are to blame, we took the responsibility, and of our own accord we marched on the wrong side.

Again, God is with us in moments of great exigencies, when we are in mighty doubt which way to turn, when opportunities come that we cannot exactly measure, at very decisive moments in our discipline. And, if we will only be guided, we shall gain the victory every time; for the opportunity is ours, the "open sesame" is upon our lips, and all we have to do is to shout out the words, and the prizes will fall into our hands. We may be deaf and dumb in the soul; we may halt between two courses, and refuse to hear the bell ringing on the right side; we may shut our eyes upon the light, and pretend to be blind. But then the blame is all our own.

My friends, look back upon the decisive hours in your lives, when, if you had turned another way, it would have been better or worse; when one way was life, the other way was death or loss or shame. And do you not now feel that a will mightier than your own, a power richer than mortals, an inspiration from Heaven, coaxed your soul along the right path; or, if you went the wrong road, a resistance, a setting aside, and a forgetfulness of higher motives, nobler impulses, and holier desires, sent you down? Oh, we sometimes say, if we had gone first in the wrong direction, we should have been conquered; and but a hair's breadth saved us. Ah! that hair's breadth was Almighty God, who is not far from any one of us. So, when we travel away from our homes, God is not far away from us, although we often feel that we never can be quite as safe anywhere as we are in our own dwelling, surrounded by our friends, guarded by our many comforts, and seemingly shielded from any accident or trouble or pain. And, when we go away from the family circle, there is a feeling of uncertainty, not only for those who are left, that for a while must care for themselves, not only for our property, that never seems so secure as when we are at hand to protect it, but also we are troubled lest in our travelling something may happen, some rail be out of place, some wheel be loosened, some foundation be weak, some bridge be broken down, some rock be in the way; and we are apt to forget that God is with us just the same in the cars, in the coach, in the public mansion, by the mountains, or by the seaside,— everywhere with us, and just as kind, good, and loving as when we are in our own dwelling, surrounded by our own dear ones, and seemingly perfectly safe from all intrusion. And we do not remember that this same God can be with our dear ones at home just as well as with us, and that he is omnipresent with his benedictions, care, and fellowship,

— not far from them, not far from us, and not far from anybody, and protecting all his children wherever they may be found.

Again, in sickness we can trace this near presence, a greater help than the powerful medicine of the skilful physician, or the careful nursing of the self-sacrificing nurse, or the patient watching of devoted friends; a power that made the medicine do its right work, that turned the nursing into a benediction, that hallowed the anxious love of dear ones, that filled the room with angelic influences and sent healing graces from the eternal city.

How did we ever get through those terrible diseases that confused the brain, paralyzed the strength, stole the flesh away, broke the nerves in pieces, and left us for a while but shadows, hardly recognized by those who knew us best? And how is it that now we are healthy and strong, as if nothing had ever touched the body and made us prostrate?

Ah! one word explains it. It is not chance, nor luck, nor skill, nor nature. No, nothing mortal; but that word is God. His voice went forth, and we arose and walked. And so, when death shall come, and when we enter heaven, and through all eternity, God will not be far away from any one of us. The greatest dread about death is, first, the thought of extinction; and, secondly, the thought that the journey is to be taken all alone,— the great future to be met without a companion. It is a seeming leap in the dark.

I suppose, if we could take away from all minds the fear of going out, expiring, ending forever, or that other dread of going alone into some unknown place, to an existence shadowy and undefined, death would be viewed only as an incident in life,— like going to a meal, making a call, and taking a journey. I know that some will say that they had rather go out than go on they know not where, either because they fear the consequences of living forever or because the other life seems like a ghost-life, and not worth the experiment; but, even then, I doubt if such people say what they mean.

Go out, go to nothing, be really no more, the "I" extinguished everlastingly? Do they prefer that?

It cannot be; for then they impeach their birth, they call in question this mortal life, they hurl a satire upon all their joys and friends, and they wrap a winding-sheet over all heaven.

Why, I had rather live as a ghost, or a fairy, or a dewdrop, than to go out. However, going out, even philosophically, is impossible; for nothing material is ever wasted, and nothing spiritual is ever thrown away.

We shall go on, and— here comes the comfort— we shall not go on alone. God is not far away: he is close by us, he will go with us; and, if he goes with us, and if we are really avowed children of God, we shall go to a good place, to a real life, to sure growth, and the other life will not be a failure.

And so through all eternity shall we be led on by

the constant Friend,— led on, if we are faithful, from splendor to splendor, from honor to honor, from glory to glory,— and experience joys, feel delights, and witness a magnificence that no words can possibly describe.

But how is it that we find the One who is not far away, how do we get at the blessed reality of his holy presence, and how can we believe these great truths, — that One is close to us, at our birth, in our temptations, at critical times, in all our journeyings, in sickness, sorrow, death, and forever and ever? For no one living to-day has seen God at any time, nor heard his voice; and is this whole discourse nothing but a pleasant dream, an idle fancy, a mirage of the mind, and the mere mist of the soul? Well, as believers in Jesus, as readers of the New Testament, as close students of the last nineteen hundred years, we have a foundation for all that we have said: we have One who stamps his holy approval on the truth of the near and dear and helping Father; and he, the Messenger of God, his image, his Son, has declared that he and his Father will dwell with all that love the truth.

The indwelling God is the great proclamation of our Lord and Saviour Jesus Christ; and "I will never leave nor forsake you" was not only said in the Old Testament, but was re-echoed when Jesus exclaimed, "Lo, I am with you always, even unto the end of the world!"

XVIII.

THE SOUL'S WEIGHT.

"Thou art weighed in the balance, and art found wanting."—DAN. v. 27.

EVERYBODY is weighed in the balances, and found wanting; for we all of us have our weak spots, so that, if the tempter could only discover the exact locality of our weakness, there would be but little hope for any one of us. But it is very fortunate, however, for a great many people that the weakest spot is never developed; and thus they are able to go through the world shielded from danger, free from disgrace, and with a very fair moral and religious reputation.

But, on the other hand, there are many persons who seem continually exposed in their most vulnerable parts, while they, on this account, always stand in the dark; and I presume that there are many men in the prison of the State no worse, perhaps not half so bad, as some outside, who stand high in society and who bask in the sunshine of popular favor.

I do not mean to say that criminals should never be punished, nor that they are to be somewhat excused because they are unfortunate; but I do mean to declare that there are many criminals roving our streets who have never received their brand, and never will till death disrobes them, till they arrive at the altar of God, and till they are ordered to give an account of their stewardship. Undoubtedly, when we are ushered into the eternal world, we shall be surprised to see how things are managed there; and we shall look for many of those who stood on earth clothed in great power and receiving the homage of the crowd, while we shall find that, in a great many cases, they are placed very low, being obscured by the brilliancy of those whom they once disdained. For our station in life here is no positive mark of the stand that we shall take hereafter. Here there may be a great deal of make-believe, a vast amount of tinsel, and considerable masquerade; but there all things will pass for what they are worth, so that no masks will avail one moment towards concealing the tremendous reality. If, then, we all have weak spots, whether we know it or not, even those the most unconscious possessing the greatest number of them, are we not taught the need of charitable construction, should we not look upon our frail fellow-beings with a sympathetic eye, and should we not treat them with all tenderness, good will, and deep sympathy, thus winning them back to righteousness, self-respect, and peace? But is this the usual way? Are we not too ready to spread an evil report, discoloring it by our imagination and imbittering it by our passions? Do we not turn away from the offender with a scornful look, crushing him or her by our contempt? Are we not barricading daily the road by which the sinful one can return to better ways, and are we not making his or her penitence almost hopeless by our severe and unsparing criticism?

Let us look well to our own hearts, purify the chambers of the inner man, sweep away the rubbish at our own doors, and be very sure that our brain and soul are thoroughly clean, ere we harshly treat an erring one; or else, before we know it, at a feast it may be, or in private, or as we walk the street, or anywhere and everywhere, we shall hear that awful voice,— the voice of conscience,— which there is no mistaking, and which cannot be easily muffled, saying, Thou, not thy neighbor; thou, who art so frightfully judging; thou, who art priding thyself upon thy holiness and thy honor, art weighed in the balances and found wanting,— wanting in a true self-judgment, wanting in charity, and wanting in many of the elements that help to form a solid Christian character.

"Who art thou that judgest another?" "Take the beam out of thine own eye, then shalt thou see clearly to take the mote from thy brother's eye." "Know thyself" is not only a Grecian, but also a Christian motto; and it is the greatest of all knowledge for us to be acquainted with our own mind, heart, and soul.

Some persons seem better acquainted with everybody and everything else rather than with themselves, and they have no plummet with which to sound their own worth, no scales with which to weigh their own merits, and no square by which to measure their own rectitude; and they forget all about the great eye that is looking on their own hearts, the eternal arch that surrounds their own souls, the inward temple where they are commanded to worship, the compass that marks off their responsibilities, and the level that would stretch their own deeds to the strict law of truth. Or, to use less figurative language, they forget all about the soul that they carry with them,— its responsibilities, its possibilities, its discipline, its glories; and they prefer to throw their neighbor into the crucible of their caustic judgment rather than to throw themselves under the full glare, the rich sifting, and the glorious consecration of Christ's precepts.

"Thou art weighed in the balances."

A man is weighed in the balances sometimes when he least expects it; for some of us — ay, many of us — in this world stand for just what we are worth, and no more; and our real character is better known than we suppose. People may praise us to our face; but they are talking all the time about us when we are absent. And I do not doubt a great many people are living with the comfortable thought that they are highly esteemed by their fellow-men, admired for their genius, praised for their courage, loved for their spasms of generosity, honored for their strict and unflinching integrity, and, in fact, rated at much above their real worth and at a mark very much above what their own souls could possibly justify. Do not let any one be deceived, my friends; for this is not often the case. Those that know us are slow to praise, and are much more ready to blame. So that, however brilliant at times we may be, we are watched at all times; and we are estimated, not by any fits of goodness, but by the ordinary current of our lives. No matter what our occasional appearance may be, if we are in our hearts miserly and in our minds jealous, ill-natured, ambitious, and vain; for all these faults will publish themselves, will be treasured up by the critics, and they will balance fearfully against our occasional explosions of goodness. Our real character betrays itself in our eye, expression, and manner; and we cannot help being detected, however much we may bow and smile, and however sacredly we may talk. Are we misers? Well, everybody knows it; for this fact is revealed in our purchases, sales, in the arrangement of our clothing, the management of our homes, the very words that we utter and the way that we utter them, in a certain twist of our lips and curve of our brow.

Are we ambitious? It is seen in the flash of our eyes, in the flush of our cheeks, and in our sensitiveness to public opinion.

Whatever we are, we carry the placard with us, with the history written out, so that the discerning ones will read it, however careful we may be.

Oh, what a startling thought is this, that we carry the proclamation of what we are right before us, just as if each one had a banner marked, "I am a miser," "I am a sensualist," "I am a thief," and "I am a murderer"! Let us be resolved that we will never carry banners of shame, but that around us shall be written, in letters of gold, "I am the Lord's."

I may be said, in these remarks, to be trespassing upon the departments of phrenology, physiognomy, physiology, and kindred sciences. Well, be it so; for there is much truth connected with these various departments of knowledge, and, wherever truth has any resting-place, there a religious philosophy is at home. For religion does not confine itself exclusively to the Bible nor to a man's mind and soul; but it goes everywhere for illustrations, power, and companionship, and it embraces all the sciences and all the arts, as far as they are penetrated with the spirit of holiness. If medical facts and spiritual realities agree, so much the better for both; for then we have a double evidence for what we wish to establish, and then there is no way of escaping the conclusions to which we come. And I believe that we can never state any great truth of God without having all nature springing up to indorse it. A man's own body chants its reality; the stars proclaim its certainty, illuminating it by their brilliant light; the forests stand guard over it, rustling with approval; and the waters embrace it, indorsing it with every sparkle, dash, foam, and tumble.

There need never be any quarrel between God's word and God's works, for they are one: they act together, and they blend their harmonies, interlace their prophecies, substantiate, enlarge, and electrify each other. And they never go alone, but each one calls out to the other for help; for both are sentinels that are appointed by the Almighty. "Thou art weighed in the balances.". We are sometimes surprised when we hear of any one who has suddenly, as we call it, committed a great crime; but we need not be so surprised, for the man only fell when attacked in the very place where he was not fortified, and he had always been weak there, but never before had been tempted.

A man may establish quite a good reputation for a long while, if only the strong points in his character are called out, if there be no abrasion of the exposed sides; and he may seem to be a hero in the eyes of all who meet him. But let a gale come on the wrong side, let the wind beat on the frail part, and place all the battering-rams of temptation against the locality where he has forgotten to fortify, and then soon he will be a wreck.

The public exclamation will be: "What a fall was there! — so good a man, so much trusted, and standing so high! Is there any reliance to be placed upon any one now, and may not all be quickly led astray?" But, if the public would only look a little deeper, they will find that this man had never been what he ought to have been, and they will see that for years he has been tottering on the brink of the precipice; for no man falls from goodness suddenly, and decay is a long while going on. We may not perceive the failure: the outside may be fair and ruddy, and the very picture of health; but down by the core we shall see corruption enough, that is waiting only the gracious opportunity for a startling manifestation.

The embryo of many a crime that has been so many years developing in secret, and has at last exploded, may have been a prevarication in childhood or a slight theft then, or an angry look, or a profane word,— all small then, and hardly worth noticing, and yet, just like the little worm in the timber of the ship, that kept working year in and year out, till at last it summoned the vessel and all its noble freight of human lives to the bottom of the ocean.

"Thou art weighed in the balances, and found wanting."

So, not very long ago, the financial power of one of the cities of the United States was weighed, and found wanting.

Credit too far extended and too thinly based, coquetting with the miser, running wild with the spendthrift, shaking hands with cunning, bowing pleasantly to fraud, making millionaires of paupers, and thrusting the rich into want,— ah! these are the things that make banks tremble everywhere, and prove a lack of prudence, foresight, honor, courage, purity, and holiness.

Ah, yes! there is a great destruction when dishonesty gains the upper hand; for then money becomes tissue paper, and the great spider's web that seems to be full of splendid threads of gold comes to pieces,— swept clean by the stern blows of reality.

My friends, the words of our text are the words of

Christianity to every one who lives. Compare the requisitions of the gospel to each one's thoughts and habits, and then see how sadly deficient we all are.

We are told "to bring every thought into subjection to Christ"; but who of us does that? We are told "that for every idle word we speak we shall be called to account"; but how many idle words do you and I speak every day of our lives? And we are ordered to make our conversation "yea, yea, and nay, nay,"—that is, as concise, truthful, and robust as possible; and do we strictly follow this law?

Ah! when we compare ourselves as we are with ourselves as we ought to be, well may each one of us exclaim, as did one of old, "Lord, be merciful to me a sinner!"

"Thou art weighed in the balances, and art found wanting."

It seems that Belshazzar, the king, made a great feast for a thousand of his lords, and took sacred vessels from the temple, in order that he and his family might use them for drinking-cups. And, while they were drinking wine, worshipping false gods, and were in the midst of their insane revelry, upon the plaster of the wall, over against the candlestick, came forth fingers of a man's handwriting, "Mene, mene, tekel, upharsin." Mene, God hath numbered thy kingdom and finished it; tekel, thou art weighed in the balances, and art found wanting; upharsin, thy kingdom is divided.

Poor old king! of what use is thy royalty now, and

what is thy feast worth? For there is a skeleton at the door, the executioner is near, judgment is at hand, and you must pay the price of all thy falsity and crime.

But, friends, everywhere now where sin is committed there is a handwriting on the wall; and it says, "Beware, repent, turn aside, look aloft, and become a new being!"

Young man, ere you touch that coin that does not belong to you, on which your eyes and your heart are so terribly cast; ere you throw the loaded dice that are to bring you an accursed fortune by the spoliation of a weak-minded adversary; and ere you drink your senses away, that you may bask in the delirium of irresponsibility,— remember, I beseech you, remember, the handwriting on the wall. Young woman, pause ere you sacrifice soul to sense, honor to expediency, and your heart to the world. For over against every step that you take, though you be ever so secret, there is a writing on the wall. Ah! let us all remember that there is no escaping Belshazzar's sentence, if we follow in Belshazzar's steps, and let us be sure that all roads are fatal but the way that leads to righteousness. Jesus Christ was weighed in the balances, and found not wanting.

Everything about him was correct, and he was the only one ever clothed in flesh in whom there was no guile. There was a perfect character, there was a finished life, there was a complete example; and only as we lean on his breast, press his hand, and follow in his steps, shall we begin to see light, rest, and peace.

The weak spot about us spoils our happiness, deranges our plans, sheds a gloom over all our hours, and makes even our virtues pale, our prayers timid, our best moments unsubstantial, and sends a rust over our ideas, benumbs our affections, palsies all our best efforts; and how shall we get rid of it? Only by the help of God, through our Lord Jesus Christ, joined to our constant endeavors.

How beautifully one has said, speaking of his own need of the Master's help,—

> "Jesus, thy loving voice I hear.
> I bow the knee
> To thy sweet spirit's power near,
> And press to thee.
> Thou leadest on to God in heaven.
> Lead on! Thou callest me.
>
> "Earth's way is long, grief tries me sore,
> I look to thee;
> And, though thorns gall my bleeding feet,
> I'll follow thee,
> Remembering that thy life was given
> To set my spirit free.
>
> "Through darkest clouds and longest night
> I'll trust in thee;
> And, when my eyes grow dim for light,
> I'll cry to thee,
> Knowing that from thy home above
> Thou wilt my comfort be."

Ah! to get rid of the spot — the weak spot in our characters — is the work of a life; and we must pray earnestly for its removal, must be unyielding to its demands, must keep it away from temptation, and stand guard over it all the time, with a Bible, a chant, and holy deeds. We must never lose sight of its presence, exposures, and power; we must call for legions of angels to surround, fortify, and cleanse it; and we must hedge it around with virtues that will be massive enough to barricade its walls forever. The weak spot will then, in time, be no longer weak; for it will gradually disappear, it will fade beautifully away, it will be subdued, conquered, overcome, and glorified. And then the peace of God will fall with great grace upon our hearts, while we shall be treading on the very boundary lines of the celestial kingdom.

XIX.

THE CHRISTIAN MARK.

"They took knowledge of them, that they had been with Jesus." — Acts iv. 13.

THERE are a great many signs by which we can almost always distinguish a truly Christian man and a really consecrated woman. The looks are a telegraph to our consciousness of some kind of a character that is in this way made eloquent; and there is something about the eye, mouth, and general expression that is apt to reveal goodness or badness right away.

I do not agree with those who say that, if one cannot look you directly in the face, there is ground for suspicion, since some of the most adroit villains will try to gaze you out of countenance, while oftentimes an exceedingly modest man or woman never can, for any length of time, keep the eyes in a straight line. Still, as you look at me, I ought to be able to have some idea as to what you are; not according to that false rule — false to the very core — that a black eye is temper, a gray one cunning, a blue one good nature, since this rule will very frequently prove entirely wrong, and a true judgment can only be formed by the general appearance, and never by any special mark.

Is the general appearance sharp or gentle, repulsive or holy, sceptical or devout, good or wicked; and does he or she look like a child of God or like a child of Satan?

Here, too, we must guard against prejudice, undue haste, and nervous sensitiveness in forming an opinion; and we must be very free from all outside influence, arriving at our decision after much study, careful thought, and a real tender, serious, and conscientious search.

So, too, by speech we find out one another; for there is something in the voice of each one of us that tells people what we are. I do not here refer to what we say and to how we say it when we are on our guard, when we are putting on our best behavior, when we want to gain the good opinion of the one with whom we converse, when we are entertaining a visitor, in our dealings with a customer to whom we wish to make large sales, and when we wish to secure favor with any one; for not then will our talk betray us. But let us look at our unguarded moments with wife and children when the doors are closed, with servants when the windows are down and company is gone, with the poor whose services are of no avail, and in moments when we throw off our mask and appear just as we are. Then are our voices a photograph of what we are, then do the angels place our pictures in the great album of heaven, and then do our tones, words, and manners declare to men and to angels just what we really are.

Of course, the best of us are at times impatient, petulant, and once in a while thoroughly excited. I do not refer to occasional infirmities, but to our general appearance when unobserved.

A great many apparently very lovely people are anything but lovely when seen in their real disposition; and a great many wives, husbands, children, fathers, and mothers could unmask for us quite a number of the people in the world who have gained the reputation of a complete saintship.

But there is something even in the tones that we generally use, and in the words that we usually employ, that will unfold a great deal of what we are; for one with gentle tones and kind words cannot be thoroughly bad, while one with a harsh voice and savage speech, who never smiles, cannot be thoroughly good. Of course, a flatterer will be weighed for the little that he is worth, a sycophant will be despised, a hypocrite will be discovered, and a poisoned honey will be at once rejected; but reality, although it be real but a few moments, will be weighed, observed, and admired.

If one should never use impure and profane language, should never tell a falsehood, should never utter a rough and an unkind word, and should always talk tenderly, purely, and believingly, why, we cannot help thinking that such a one possesses a great many noble traits of character, that are worthy of our deepest regard.

So, too, if one be always profane, untrue, unholy,

light and every way loose in conversation, we cannot help feeling and saying that such a one appears to be far, very far, from the kingdom of heaven, and seems to need very much the grace of Almighty God for a complete sanctification. So, too, by deeds we judge of a person; and this way of judging seems more safe, generous, and catholic than any other. Unfortunate circumstances may affect one's gaze and voice, and may make rough one's talk, so that really very good persons at the core of the heart may be very unpromising in all their outward manifestations, — like some splendid nuts, that really are very rough to the handling and exceedingly unpromising on the outside, but grandly good in the meat.

"By their fruits shall ye know men," was said by the one who possessed the highest wisdom.

Of course, the one who steals, lies, murders, and disobeys the "Decalogue" in any one particular, cannot be a thoroughly good person. A knave may have a beautiful eye, an open countenance, an attractive manner, and an oily voice; and yet he is nothing but a knave, after all, — just as some of our most ruddy apples are found not good for much after the skin is removed.

Of course, the one who is all the time going about doing good, whom the poor bless and the distressed almost worship, cannot be labelled utterly bad. And so the one who never does any good, whom no one loves, and whom the poor and distressed thoroughly distrust, — that one must be bad, even if he or she should have the face of an angel and the voice of a seraph.

What we are doing reveals to God, to man, and to all heaven and earth what we really are.

If you claim the name of Christian, before I grant your claim I must ask you, What are you doing in the house, street, shop, office, and at the exchange? What are you doing, my brother and my sister, for the growth of the soul, the good of your fellow-men, and for your advance towards heaven? Are you always, in every small item, in sight or out of sight, trying with all your might and main to live strictly on the square?

If you were to tell me about any one's being particularly good, I should beg leave to propound the following questions in regard to him or her: —

How is Sunday spent by the one of whom you speak,— in sleep or in church, in pleasure or in devotion, doing good or trying to kill time, as a burden or as a privilege? Yet more would I ask, How are all the days spent? For one day good and six days bad will bring a most terrible satire upon our make-believe Christianity. Are all the days somehow consecrated to truth, honor, and holiness? Is God kept very near continually? Does he or she walk with Jesus all the time? Is the sense of a glorious responsibility kept ever bright; and would the right arm be sacrificed before a wrong thought would be cherished, a wicked word be spoken, and a bad deed be performed; and is the perfume of sanctity continually exhaled from everything and all things that are connected with the daily life? How is good fortune met,— thankfully, modestly, and religiously? How is bad fortune met,— cheerfully, humbly, hopefully, sweetly, sacredly, and triumphantly? How is an insult taken,— patiently, tenderly, lovingly, and in a forgiving spirit? When sickness comes, or bereavement, or death, what is done? Is there resignation, faith, courage, devotion, and a joyous surrendering of the human will, or, rather, a beautiful blending of it with the divine appointment?

Have you seen your friend under all circumstances, pleasing or sad, and found that the heart was true in every vicissitude? We know very well that some people are very good, happy, attractive, and splendid Christians, to all appearances, under success and when everything goes well, who are just the opposite when bad days come.

A great many bear their successes very beautifully, — never complain about receiving a large income, never are troubled by a multitude of friends, have very splendid tempers in their palatial homes, and seem thoroughly satisfied with their many comforts; and yet we have, at such times, no true test of the real character of such ones. Nor can we ever get a just estimate as long as the golden streams continue to flow. But let a reverse come, let a storm arrive, let the income stop, let the beautiful house be sold, let those who have had enough or more than enough be reduced to a sad poverty, and will they say, and can they say, as Job did once: "The Lord gave, and the Lord hath taken away. Blessed be the name of the Lord"?

If they can thus bend sweetly, grandly, and gloriously, then they are saints, indeed; but, if they grow morose, discontented, unhappy, and unholy, they simply prove that all their seeming gentleness was built upon a very poor foundation.

We all most especially need, in our hours of prosperity, the help of Almighty God. Do you say, "Pray for the poor; for they need it, and that is about all that they can get"?

Well, my favored friend, I will pray for them, but much more for you; for you need it much more in your abundance. For your temptations must of necessity be very great, your responsibility must be very mighty; and you need, above all, the grace of the Father, that you may worthily enjoy and use your great and glorious privileges.

A truly good, solid, and genuine character is always independent of circumstances, and is right royal in a palace or in a hut, in sickness or in health, in life or in death, in time or in eternity.

Heap every comfort upon true souls, and you will not be able to change their spirit out of modesty into pride, out of humility into ambition, out of devotion into self-seeking, and out of God into the world.

Or take everything away from such, the spirit will be the same: it will not swerve from gentleness into discontent, from peaceableness into anger, from trust into misanthropy, from joy into sadness, and from worship into atheism. No, no! For the soul will sing just as sweetly in the cage as in the forest, and it will make every hideous cross a magnificent crown.

"They took knowledge of them, that they had been with Jesus."

If we, then, have kept company with Jesus, how shall we show it, and where are the proofs of our royal companionship?

It will be detected in our patience, gentleness, courage, piety, and holiness.

Certainly, one of the greatest virtues of the really good man or woman is patience; for all need its beautiful blessing, at all times and everywhere.

Husbands and wives with each other, parents with their children, brothers and sisters together, friends and neighbors, the seller and the buyer,—all need it, and a great deal of it, every day that life shall last.

We can place our finger on some homes, and say, All that is wanted just there is patience; and this is the cause of all the care, misunderstanding, mistakes, and troubles, and, this being given, the "Babel" would become a "Bethel."

We can point to neighborhoods and exclaim, A little more forbearance would make everything more bright and beautiful in all these hearts,—would stop ill-feeling, check harsh words, smother miserable misunderstandings, and start up a generous and noble self-denial, hastening the kingdom of God.

So we might look at the various places of trade, and prove that the lack of patience is the cause of the many losses, the much unhappiness, and the great revolutions that are constantly taking place. So the same might be said about gentleness, courage, piety, and holiness; for all these graces of character are much needed for the ripening of the true soul, and they all must be put in practice for the upbuilding of the kingdom of God, for they make happy families, healthy communities, solid governments, and tend to hasten the time "when the lion and the lamb shall recline together."

But all these graces, in their sure perfection, are found but in one character,—even in "the Lamb of God, who takes away the sin of the world."

In him alone is seen a patience that never grows tired, a gentleness that becomes more bright in the most trying times, a courage all the more splendid when seemingly the most beset, a piety that no mockery can quench, and a holiness which not the bitterest enemy can impeach.

Look at him, the Son of God, for your example, life, help, victory, and coronation.

Paul Gerhard has said, and with some of his beautiful words let us close,—

"A Lamb goes uncomplaining forth,
  The guilt of all men bearing,
Laden with all the sin of earth,
  None else the burden sharing.
Goes patient on, grows weak and faint,
To slaughter led without complaint,
  That spotless life to offer.
Bears shame and stripes and wounds and death,
Anguish and mockery, and saith,
  Willingly all this I suffer.

"My life-long days would I still thee
  Be steadfastly beholding,
Thee ever, as thou ever me,
  With loving arms enfolding.
And, when my heart grows faint and chill,
My heart's undying light, oh, still
  Abide unchanged before me.
Myself thy heritage I sign,
Ransomed to be forever thine,
  My only hope and glory.

"And, when at last thou leadest me
  Into thy joy and light,
Thy blood shall clothe me royally,
  Making my garments white,
Shall place upon my head the crown,
Shall lead me to the Father's throne,
  And raiment fit provide me,
Till I, by him to thee allied,
By thee, in costume like a bride,
  Stand modestly beside thee."

XX.

THE GRACE OF GOD.

"By the grace of God, I am what I am."— 1 COR. xv. 10.

AT this present time people are apt to forget, or to ignore, or to deny, or to muffle the thought that they are what they are on their best side, in their most prosperous moments, and at the acme of their holiest success, by the grace of Almighty God. And, in fact, a great many people seem to say, or to imply, or to want everybody else to think that they are what they are by the power of their own right arm, by the brilliancy of their imagination, by the keenness of their wit, by the clearness of their reason, and by some great personal exploit that is based on their own will; and they seem to say, Look at us, not at God; for our right hand has gotten us the victory,— that is to say, this is an age of scepticism, a time when many are shutting out the divine impetus, force, spirit, and power: it is the hour of the exaltation of man, the deification of nature, and the worship of second causes. And I am not at all alarmed as to the ultimate result of all these questionings, self-assertions, and high-handed claims; and, although I have no sympathy with, and a natural recoil from, and a freezing antipathy to, many and to almost all of the statements of those who take these claims and push them before our notice, and give public lectures that they may be notorious, yet, I repeat, I am not alarmed, nor confused, nor in any way seriously troubled. For the whole thing seems to be an approach to God from the wrong side, but, nevertheless, an approach to God that must ultimately bring the great First Cause near, and convince the most sceptical mind that he is near, precious, and all-controlling.

A denial of a self-evident truth will always end in the explosion of the denial, in the building up of the truth on the most prominent part of the soul, in the glorious reaction of the sceptical spirit, and in the planting of the ladder of faith on the battlements of heaven.

If I should stand before a stately edifice,—beautiful in proportion, imposing in appearance, rich in material, showing wondrous skill inside and outside, the admiration of all eyes, and the pride of all hearts, —I should be surprised, of course, if that edifice, being able to speak, should say, I am self-created, and I all alone threw all these stones into place, raised up this noble structure, created everything that is grand about myself; and I demand that all praise and gratitude and applause and respect shall be given to myself. I should be surprised, I say, at such a talk, at such an assumption, and at such a daring challenge upon common sense; but I should not be overpowered, nor convinced, nor converted. But I should wait until the building got out of repair, till it began to shake and to tremble, till the stones crumbled, the walls leaned, and a general spirit of decay was apparent. And I should then ask the old worn-out, dilapidated, and miserable wreck to repair itself, to work its own renovation, to leap back to its own beauty, and to show a resurrection of its former power. What you have done once, I should exclaim, do again; for, according to your former faith, no builder is needed but yourself, and no architect but your own skill, and no brain but your own wit, and please repeat now the miracle that you have claimed simply rested in your own keeping. Then would be the hour of my religious triumph; and then the building would demand a builder, call out for a restorer, piteously seek for an outside power, or else, by falling to the ground, would proclaim its own impotency, falsity, and fearful mistake.

When we shut out the grace of Almighty God, my friends, and build on our own foundation, or claim so to do, and hold up our own flag, blow our own trumpet, announce our personal claims, and place the everlasting "I" upon a golden throne,— then, when the sky is blue, times are propitious, the gales are easy, and all seems well,— then, oh, then, our pride, our self-assertion, and our personal esteem appear to master everybody and to conquer all things. But let a storm come, thunder and lightning, a fearful tempest, heavy sickness, terrible losses, stinging pains, and the summons to depart, then very seldom, not once in a thousand times,— nay, not once in ten thousand times, — do we stand up smiling, boasting, arrogant, and say, Look at my right arm, gaze at my clear eye, worship my keen judgment, compliment my superior wisdom; and now look and behold how I can manage myself, and cure, comfort, and support myself. Oh, no! there is no such conversation then, but most likely the words, "God be merciful to me a sinner!" "Lord, I believe: help thou mine unbelief!" "Why hast thou forgotten me?" "Why go I thus heavily, while the enemy oppresseth me?" "Make haste, O God, to help me!"

Ah! how often, when the crust is thoroughly broken, the real, beating, throbbing, loving, believing heart is found! When the crust of selfishness, envy, ambition, pride, and egotism is shattered, then adamant faith is kindled, the tender embers of the soul are roused up, and the real heart is published. "By the grace of God, I am what I am." Saint Paul's experience in this respect was not peculiar; and, however varied his history, strange his trials, wonderful his escapes, and grand his teachings, here he meets us all, and here, in our own biographies, at our most solemn moments, in our most critical experiences, we can cry out that the power that upheld Saint Paul is all the time upholding us.

I ask you at this holy time to review your lives somewhat, — not aloud, not for our hearing, not for any printed record, not as a boast, but secretly, penitently, tenderly, and solemnly review your lives, and look at the steps that you have taken, the paths you have trod, the discipline you have received, the preserving, tutoring, shaping, and glorifying of the Eternal One, and see if it be not wholly by God's grace that you are where you are, that you have done the good things you have frequently done, and have passed through the cloud, the fire, and the smoke undestroyed.

Trace your childhood, those hours of wonderful escapes, of merciful supervision, of strange temptations, of peculiar dangers, and of utter helplessness, when the counsel of parents would not help, nor the guidance of friends, nor the rebukes of strangers; when you were apparently left all alone, standing on a straw over chasms of terrible depths. And yet you were not alone, you were not unprotected, you were not unwatched; for one eye was looking, one hand was guiding, one arm was upholding, one spirit was saving, and the straw held you up, and you did not fall, you did not even grow dizzy. And you said, without even knowing how you said it, "Get thee behind me, Satan!"

Ah! the rescuing of boys and of girls from ten thousand calamities seems to me one of the most grand, touching, and overwhelming proofs of the constant grace of God; and the great wonder is not that we are here, grown-up men and women, but that we ever escaped from infancy or from our childish years, when the booming shot was pouring around us with unceasing velocity, and we were with hardly any power to provide a shield and to cover our heads in the day of battle, and scarcely able to escape to a place of shelter. O mothers, precious mothers, I would not have you anxious, and in tears, and brooding over possible or probable troubles that your loved ones may meet; but I would have you rejoice, and rejoice forever in the grace of Almighty God, that never leaves our children, that besets them behind and before, that overarches them with a beauty, a glory, and a splendor that human language cannot adequately describe, according to the promise, "When thou passest through the waters, 'I' will be with thee." Again, my friends, trace your lives, since you have entered upon manhood or womanhood, and see if you cannot each one of you exclaim, "By the grace of God I am what I am."

I sometimes think that, if the choice could have been given to us to be or not to be,— and of course that supposition is logically impossible, since we must be, in order to hear the question put,— yet admit that we could be questioned, and at the same time see the possible pitfalls in our path, should we not reply, and should we not reply quickly, earnestly, and eloquently, We dare not run the risk of existence, we cannot sail safely between Scylla and Charybdis; and, oh, save us the risk! For we vastly prefer not to be. And yet, as we look at our lives, we find how graciously, how beautifully, and how grandly the interposing hand of God has led us along. Suppose that this very day we could read in print the dream of our lives as we dreamed our dream at twenty-one, — what we would do, what we should do, and what nothing could stop us from doing; the prizes that would be ours, the gains we would win, the honors wear, the respect receive, the affections challenge, and all the mighty splendors manage, — how like a fairy-tale would the account read, — calling up smiles, evoking tears, challenging laughter, and forcing out criticism. And then, suppose again, that opposite to each page our real life should be given in contrast, item by item and day by day. One side we thought to do this, and on the other side we actually did that; one side the idea, and on the other side the performance; here the beautiful castle in the air, and there the real castle on the ground. Why, sometimes the contrast would be terribly painful, at other times sweetly joyous, and at all times wonderfully strange, suggestive, and startling, — what we wanted to do, oftentimes a bubble in the air; and what we have done, frequently a sad, an agonizing, and a stern reality. But, through that reality, — again I repeat it, always would I repeat it, let the echo go through time and eternity! — we see the merciful hand of God, the grace of the Eternal One, and the splendors of a restraining love.

We are all of us, as a general rule, where we never expected to be and in situations greater or less than we ever thought possible could be filled by us, and with a power in the community widely known or hardly felt, in a way beyond any of our poor guessing, and morally or spiritually giants or dwarfs, and showing marks of hard service, of great battles, of mighty pains, and of a rough experience. And sometimes — ay, frequently — these truths can be traced in photographs that are taken of us when we were children as compared with photographs that are taken of us in matured life.

"By the grace of God, I am what I am."

Saint Paul said that; and no man could have said it more truly, more eloquently, and with a greater effect upon the minds of the people of his age and of all ages.

He began his life as a Jew, and as one of the most severe of the Jews, — a Pharisee of the Pharisees, a bigot, a cynic, and a persecutor; and he would probably have talked at that time in words like these: There is no true body of people save the Jews, and especially the Pharisees; there is no real church but the Church of Moses. The Christians are infidels; and our duty towards this infatuated people is to persecute and to kill them continually; for, verily, thus shall we do God's service. I, Saul, am one of the best of men, and one of the most zealous of believers. I have had my seat at the feet of Gamaliel. I understand the law and the prophets, and the spoken and the unspoken word; and you can hardly find a fault in my whole life.

Listen to another man, or, rather, to another kind of a man, and hear him talk.

He says: "For we preach not ourselves, but Christ

Jesus the Lord, and ourselves your servants, for Jesus' sake."

He says: "I am the least of all the apostles . . . chosen out of due season."

He cries out, "To live is Christ, to die is gain." What a different man, we say! And yet, by the grace of Almighty God, the two are one,—the same person at different stages of growth; the young man, unripe fruit,—hard, green, and sour; and the more experienced saint, the autumnal gift,—rich, juicy, luscious, and nourishing; the young man eaten up by self, and the old man filled with God; the young man preaching about his own right arm, and the older one holding up the cross of Christ; the younger one a sceptic,—proud of his intellect, revelling in his superiority, and proclaiming his zeal,—but the other one, the old man, bowing low before Almighty God, proclaiming a complete submission to the Lord, and walking through life with a thorough simplicity, a loving sincerity, and a blessed holiness.

Both these men the same, did I say? I take back my words: I beg their pardon, and I beg your pardon. The one, the younger, had not the real spirit of God; and the other, the elder, declared of himself that he was not the same as in youth; for he said, "I am a new creature," and added, "in Christ Jesus the Lord." Yes, here is the profound mystery, the glorious annunciation, and the comforting reality,—that Saint Paul became, that we can all of us become, renewed in Christ.

It only remains then for me to ask you, each one, Are you, by the grace of God, new creatures in Christ Jesus the Lord; and have you given your hearts to the Saviour, your souls to God, and your lives to holiness? May every one be able to say, Amen and amen!

XXI.

PLEASANT WORDS.

"Pleasant words are as an honeycomb, sweet to the soul." — Prov. xvi. 24.

I HARDLY think that a greater truth could have been uttered than the one here set forth in the proverb, while it is delightful for us to think that thousands of years ago people liked the gentle voice and the gracious speech quite as well as they do to-day. It is really very strange, when we all of us know the advantages, the comforts, and the joys that spring from a mild mouth that we so constantly refuse to put honey upon our lips. I believe that a great deal of our lack of success in life can be traced to our rough voice, while I know many a man, and also many a woman, who owe all the good fortune and all the high station that they enjoy to a wonderful facility of winning expression, to a peculiar suavity of tone, and to a splendid tenderness in shaping words.

Notice families; and you will easily see where they keep an Æolian harp all the time, and where they keep an instrument out of tune, discordant, harsh, and every way repulsive. Bright eyes are in the one place, a merry face, a radiant manner, and everything peaceful and holy; but in the other place you see scowls, thunder-clouds, tight lips, and a very strained and unnatural manner. Why, "please," and "thank you," and "I am much obliged" are words often heard in the one place; but "go," "come," "do this," "do that," and "take this," or "take that," are words quite familiar to the house out of tune. Why, one house seems to be filled with angels, but the other home seems encompassed by bad spirits. I read of a home once that a good mother and cheerful daughter made just as happy as they could, after the bad father was removed to the safer care of the public. This is the story as it was told: "A citizen of Detroit was sent to the house of correction. The wife, a hard-working woman and sorely afflicted, managed to provide food and fuel for herself and child, until all at once death suddenly put an end to her kind ministrations. The little girl, hardly eight years old, was all alone in the house when her mother died. The event occurred at dark, and at midnight the child was heard singing in the darkness. A pedestrian who stopped near the house heard her say, 'Mother, won't you wake up and light the lamp? If you will, I will sing some more.' Suspecting what had happened, he roused some of the neighbors; and, as they went in, the child sat in the darkness holding its mother's cold hand and singing,—

"'The Lord will lead a little child,
And teach me how to pray.'

"A dark room, death on the bed, poverty, hunger, and cold to make her situation more desolate; and yet the child of shadows was not afraid. She said: 'I kept still a long while to let mother sleep. Then I sang all my songs to keep myself awake. Then I looked out of the window, and didn't move, so that the angels wouldn't be afraid to come and talk to mother and make her smile.'" So you see that little girl did all she could to make home happy.

Why, my dear friends, pleasant words at home make all the rough places easy, all the sad hours sweetly sacred, and all the human hearts there gathered buoyant and beautiful.

We hear a great deal to-day about the huge number of divorces that are granted in this country; and, without doubt, some of the separations are such as are ordained by God. But the list is perfectly fearful, causing all who love their fellow-beings and who desire the supremacy of the Christian religion to see what can be done to stay this terrible tide of wrong. Yet I really think that the remedy for the difficulty in some of these cases is a great deal more simple, and certainly more sacred, than any help that the law affords: let one of the parties, or, if possible, both husband and wife, for one month resolve each to see which one will be the more yielding, which one will have the more musical voice, and which one will conquer the other by exquisite tenderness and by a thorough self-denial, then, in nine cases out of ten, they will not ask again to be put apart, but will hold fast to their affection till the higher call of Heaven severs the human fellowship.

It is said that there was once a certain place in which, being visited by a husband or a wife, it would be revealed which of the two would die first.

A couple believing in the superstition, and each out of peace with the other and each wishing the other's quick departure, unbeknown to the other, went at twilight to the famous spot, that, if possible, the tortured mind might be helped by finding itself a widower or a widow. The face of the one who would first go to the eternal home would, according to rumor, rise up to the vision of the questioner. Now, it so happened that these two unhappy ones went by different roads, so that, when they arrived at the enchanted ground, they faced each other. Each thought they saw a spirit, and each gladly supposed that the other was to go within a year. So they returned home silent, but joyful.

A year was so short, the husband thought he would do his best to be kind and obliging; while the wife, on the same ground, was just as sweet and just as gentle as she could possibly be, till both, as the time drew near, regretted the departure of the other, and were relieved to find the hour pass without a death.

Ever afterwards, of course, they were a loving couple, never wishing each other out of the way.

Ah! this is but another way of showing the power of mutual self-sacrifice, and it is but an illustration of the might of pleasant words. So, too, the rule

holds good in our intercourse with our neighbors. I think, perhaps, as a general rule, that a great many of the people of New England are a little too severe in manner and in speech, and are a little too frosty, critical, and self-asserting, and lack somewhat the suavity, the address, and the complaisance of the people of the other States. Not but that our hearts are as warm, deep, and gushing as the hearts of any one; but our lips are frozen, and there is too much starch in our words. We have altogether too little in New England of genuine neighborly intercourse. The satire of one of our leading preachers is somewhat deserved, even if it be a little sharp. "I walked," he says, "one evening around the streets surrounding my home; and there was but very little light in the various dwellings, and everything looked cheerless, while, if I ventured to ring the bell and ask for the family, the servant looked upon me as if I were an intruder."

Ah! I fear we all of us live too much by ourselves, have but a cold bow and icy words for those we meet, and live and die as if the world were made for us and for ours, and as if all other persons were here by mistake.

Yet just suppose a moment that one of our families were all. I care not which one; but just imagine that to-morrow morning the members of one of these families walk out finding no other soul living, every house without a tenant and every shop without a keeper, no vehicles in motion, — for there would be no one to manage them,—everything still as the grave. In such a case, how would such a family feel? Why, all the members of it would pray God before night to send the people back again. Their agony would be intense, and their self-reproach for lack of sociability would rise up in fearful clouds. They would vow a great and holy vow never again to be so seclusive, and never again to narrow their circle of friendships.

Ah! why need we wait till such a day of dire calamity? Why not now reform our manners, why not now inundate our speech with the holiest jets of celestial sweetness, and why not now love everybody, and let everybody know that we love them?

Again, in trade I plead for pleasant words. I deem, too, that this part of my subject is exceedingly important and vital, both for those who sell and for those who buy. How often you all have said, "I never will go into that store again, because they are so rough and so disobliging"! Why, every month there are hundreds of dollars lost because salesmen are so severe.

I would give a hint to all our merchants and to all our clerks that I believe invaluable, would true success be gained. I would say to them, Cultivate a pleasant voice, learn to have the patience of Job, and study to be obliging, good-natured, and self-sacrificing. I do not ask any one to be a hypocrite: I do not ask you to bow and bow with iron at your heart, and I do not want honey on your lips and vinegar on your soul; but I wish you to try both to feel and to exhibit a kindly temper and a genial spirit. I wish you to make every one who enters your place of business feel better for the visit. I insist upon it, this can be done.

I have a word for officials also at this time. I have sometimes thought — and, if you find that I am wrong, please correct me at some future time — that all those who hold a place of power, either under the government of the United States or under the various governments of New England, at the various "banks" and the "courts of justice," were not almost and altogether angels and archangels in temper. While some men are a glorious exception, who hold office with a sweetness thoroughly consoling, there are others that a little might make despots.

I call here publicly for their immediate removal, for they are unworthy of the place that they so fearfully desecrate. I would have this week every person who is not a thorough gentleman, to the poor as well as to the rich, immediately degraded; for it is high time that, in this respect, we all of us stood up for common justice. I think that it would be well for the poet to write on a great many hearts those good old words: —

> "Speak gently, let not harsh words mar
> The good you might do here.
> Speak gently, it is better far
> To rule by love than fear."

"Pleasant words are as an honeycomb, sweet to the soul." I think that we are more affected by gentle tones and gracious words than we are apt to think.

In one of the books published in France a few years ago — that contained, perhaps, some things that never should have been written, and yet gave voice to many noble thoughts that culled from the whole volume and published by themselves would have helped a large number of souls — we find this sentence, —

"The women working in the fields, the vintagers at labor among the grapes, the meek-eyed cows looking over the stone fences, the team of bullocks drawing a timber wagon wearily along, the children filling a pitcher at the roadside water-spout, the old women resting under the wayside crosses, — all had words from him, — words which left them brighter, braver, happier than they had been before those kindly eyes, shining so lustrous in the sun, had fallen on them. Man and child, woman and animal, felt the influence of glance and word as the languid flowers feel the dew, as the shaded fruit feels the summer warmth."

Thus we see this man, here described, by his pleasant face and genial words created a contagion of happiness wherever he went.

The female race gain their chief power by gentle speech. I know very well that that which most attracts man towards woman is what she says and how she says it.

A handsome face is very well as far as it goes, but

it is worth nothing without a splendid utterance; and the homeliest face looks beautiful when the lips are filled with sweetness and covered with strength.

So I would say to the gentle ones, If you wish to convert the world, if you wish to make us poor men much better and much holier than we are, if you wish to build up the Church, if you wish to spread Christianity everywhere, and if you wish to sanctify the whole earth, oh, cultivate a gracious and a holy way of speaking, and let nothing but pearls and diamonds leap out of your hearts. Then I think that woman would be clothed with true glory, would fill a place highest of all, and could preach, practise, and argue at home as well as in the "pulpit," or at the "bar," or as surgeon, or as physician; for, then, would she be a splendid lever, lifting all our souls to glory. Sisters, are you aware of your mighty power? Christian kindness, politeness, gentleness, chivalry, holy tenderness with everybody, should be the great law of our lives. A great many years ago there was a teacher who always made a bow to his pupils when he entered the school-room; and he was severely ridiculed by the other teachers, who thought by so doing he forgot his dignity and authority. But he said to those teachers, "I always bow to my pupils, because before me may be future governors, professors, generals, and emperors." Well, my friends, in that class of boys was one whose name was Martin Luther.

Once more, Jesus of Nazareth was one gracious in his speech. All men were astonished at this his mighty power; and even his bitterest enemies were held back a long while from doing him harm, owing to the force of his lips. Oh, how I would like to have heard him speak such words as these! "Neither do I condemn thee: go in peace"; "I am the good shepherd"; "I will not leave you comfortless"; "Father, forgive them! for they know not what they do." Ah! all his words were beautiful, and all his tones were sweet and sacred. He knew just how to speak and just what to say. Let us all, then, become more gentle, let us all study to be more quiet, let us not get too much excited, let us think twice before speaking once; and may all that we utter be full of the perfume of heaven. With the words of a friend I will close: —

WE MAY NOT TELL.

BY CHAS. WM. BUTLER.

We may not tell what hidden power
Lies in the present living hour,
Nor how the words therein we speak
May keep the strong and soothe the weak,
Nor how our deeds have might to thrall
Or bless the mightiest of us all;
How smiles of love or flashing scorn
Bring daylight's gleams or evening's on;
How smallest look of ours may lift
Or send a soul out sea, adrift,
May give affliction's tides to swell,
Or lands of peace wherein to dwell.
We may not tell, we may not tell.

XXII.

SPIRITUAL CLIMBING.

"O God, set me up on high."— Ps. lxix. 29.

THERE are certain sayings that become fastened to the mind and heart of us all, and always seem to be full of clear, uplifting, and sparkling truths; and among these varied sayings of our ancestors and of ourselves there is one that is to be found that seems to throw light upon the words of our text. It is this: that "nothing ever stands still." Truly, there must be growth, upward or downward, for the better or for the worse; and we are all the time either going forward or backward, for we can never keep quiet. The difference each day may be imperceptible, but it is sure;.and there never were two men, nor two trees, nor two days, nor two stars, nor two flowers, nor two rain-drops, nor two snow-flakes alike, nor any one of these the same to-day that it was yesterday.

This constant motion that affects us one and all is meant for an encouragement as well as for a warning, and is ordained to help, and not to harm us. For the clouds in the sky as they sail along, the trees as they rustle, the waters as they ebb, your pulse as it beats, and the world as it swings in space, making its punctual circuit around the sun,—all these seem to articulate,—oh, so sweetly and grandly!—Ascend, advance, conquer!

As we study all the ages, we shall find ample evidence of the progressive law; for, whether we begin with Eden and its two inhabitants, who at first knew only enjoyment, or come down to the present day, viewing the billions who dwell upon the earth, who understand sorrow, duty, and discipline as well as joy, we shall clearly see "advance" engraved on every century, and we shall detect a rich development in science, ethics, and theology.

The first parent was created perfectly innocent; but he did not know everything, else he never could have sinned, and he would have been divine. If we allow that Adam was a man, we must look upon his knowledge as limited; and thus we find in the very commencement of creation a way opened for growth.

Genesis is but the beginning, as the name betokens; Exodus is a disclosure, or an advance; the Apocalypse is a revelation of what is to be; and the whole Bible seems to utter those pungent words, "Go forward," "More yet to be revealed," "Every hour a growth," from Moses to Isaiah, on to Christ, who himself said, "The Comforter is to come," and on to the apostles, who still pointed to a future and to a second coming of Christ, and who exclaimed with eloquence, "Press forward!"

We find, as we study the Bible,—nor need the assertion be considered as any impeachment of its glorious inspiration,— that the science of Moses was only in its infancy, and that his theology was such as Jesus thought fit to correct. For, if Moses had attained to perfection in all points, the New Testament would be of no use and Judaism would have sufficed. But, really, the second revelation is the extension, growth, and improvement of the first.

The New Testament starts grand principles, lifts up to view majestic facts, and reveals wonderful and astonishing precepts, that will demand a forever for a complete obedience. One dispensation says, "An eye for an eye and a tooth for a tooth"; but the better Testament exclaims, "Forgive your enemies, and bless those who curse you, and pray for those who despitefully use you and treat you." And the people of the earth have hardly got free from the first command, while it will be ages yet before they will fully understand the second, the rim of which they have scarcely yet grazed. If we take a view of theology as it buds and blossoms through the ages, what vast changes we behold!

God is always the same, but he is not always apprehended alike.

Idolatry shapes him in a block, atheism fastens him to fate, pantheism enshrines him in universality, Judaism cages him in justice and shuts him up in law, and Christianity engirdles him in all things good and lovely; and yet the Christian idea is far ahead of the general thought, and it calls upon the race "to go up higher" in their conceptions and to keep grasping more and more clearly celestial realities. Again, let us remember that every man who grows helps others to grow, and that every biography of a noble man that is given to the world is a benefit to the race. For thus is the road to virtue made more easy, thus are bridges thrown over the difficulties that oppose us, thus are all of us urged to march on and to march up, and thus are beacon lights thrown in our way, so that we may find the true harbor, and so that dangerous rocks and fearful shoals may be revealed, so that on the heart a radiant light may shine, and on the will a new energy may fall.

There is a book published entitled "The Christian and Social Life," while the aim of this work is to sketch for public admiration the characters of Howard, Wilberforce, Budgett, Foster, Arnold, and Chalmers. One is styled the type of philanthropy; another is called its development; the third is labelled the Christian merchant; while the others are spoken of as noble specimens of men, who had risen above doubt and above despair into the ripeness and the richness of holiness. Now, do not such men, as we scan their lives, become ladders to us, by which we can climb nearer to heaven? Are not their hands outstretched, that we may be aided in our ascent to glory? Have they not dropped their mantles for our catching? and do they not breathe their choice benedictions, even upon our most feeble efforts? Can we read of goodness without exclaiming, I also am a man? My capacities can be thus enlarged, my will can be thus magnetized, and my soul may also be rendered fragrant. For God has given to me also the power to become a hero or a heroine, and he has given to me the invitation and the incentives. I can, like Howard, visit prisoners, and scatter blessings, and plead, suffer, and die for the race. I can, like Wilberforce, devote my life for the oppressed, my genius for those in bonds, my whole influence — no matter what the opposition — for those whom man subjects. I can become the Christian merchant, the princely donor, the father of hospitals and of libraries, the friend of grateful mechanics, and the fountain of life to trade and the Church. Or, like Foster, Arnold, and Chalmers, I can wade through distrust, scepticism, and a narrow and a restricted life to the firmest faith, the largest visions, and to a real, earnest, and Christian manhood. I can make all men my brothers, Jesus my Master, and God my Father.

Longfellow says, and we often sing the words in our Sunday-school: —

> "Whene'er a noble deed is wrought,
> Whene'er is spoken a noble thought,
> Our hearts in glad surprise
> To higher levels rise.

> "The tidal wave of deeper souls
> Into our inmost being rolls,
> And lifts us unawares
> Out of all meaner cares.

"Honor to those whose words or deeds
Thus help us in our daily needs,
And by their overflow
Raise us from what is low."

Yes, my friends, biography charms, quickens, and elevates us. For good men and good women live not only for themselves, but also for others; and every noble deed is infinite in its noble consequences, and heaven is all the more easy of access because up the heights that lead there have marched, in glorious and triumphant procession, the hosts of the obedient, loving, generous, and holy,— because up that illuminated road have passed patriarch, prophet, apostles, and martyrs. Saintly men, holy women, and lovely children all have made the way to God attractive; and they have also made this world, which is the portico and the outward gate to heaven, more full of meaning and more rich in prophecy. What an encouragement this is, that we should anoint our lives with holiness! and what a reward for us, if we do well, that our deeds are prolific, and that their fragrance spreads from century to century, from heart to heart, and from earth to heaven!

We ought to go forward and to pray God to set us up on high, so that others may go up, and so that all may be saved. When we come to the life of Jesus, what a mountain height we view, what attractive slopes, and what rich verdure! Up higher, this character says,— not higher than my heights, for that would not be possible, but nearer and ever nearer to my summit, although you never reach it, and although it always seems to be inaccessible. Deeper into the wisdom of his life, closer into the glory of his precepts, more intimately into the richness of his deeds, more grandly into the solemnity, humility, and majesty of his departure, and more devoutly into the certainty, purity, and sublimity of his presence we are to travel, and to travel on as new light bursts upon us, as radiance is heaped upon radiance, majesty is encircled within majesty, and the splendor of manhood, the glory of Divinity, and the attractiveness of sonship are all made known to the wondering ears and the seeking hearts of the children of God.

Perfection should always prove a spur, and never a check, to our growth; and we should not be chilled and bewildered by goodness, but ever aided, always strengthened, and gloriously consecrated.

Like the sun, let goodness penetrate, warm, and vivify the objects that it visits. So, when we gaze upon the Son of God, let us not be driven to flight by the magnitude of his glory; but let us rather be won onward and upward, be lifted out of our low desires, braced with new principles, ashamed of our imperfect lives, glad to escape from the tyranny of sin, and all ready and very joyous to claim friendship, fellowship, and discipleship with one who was without guile and without stain.

We are told to "mount upwards," but really, and not artificially; not in haste, unprepared; not in pride, hollow at the heart; not without a consecrated purpose, and not without a good foundation. For the advance is not to be in our professions alone, but in our practice, and not to be made known so much by our outward position as by our inward life. For we are to be, and not to seem; and we are to claim no quality of goodness that will not stand the test, lest in the day of trial our false position should be revealed, and all our virtue be found decayed at the core. Too many persons stand above reality: they are rated for more than their spiritual worth. They are pyramids in society, when in real size and actual weight they are terribly belittled; and the very base of the pyramid is erected on marshy ground, that in time will give way and shatter the whole monument.

Also there are many persons who, like the prairie rose, blush for a time unseen and publish their beauty to the desert air, until perchance some traveller plucks the flower, admires its peculiar and rich color, rejoices in its delicacy, and ever spreads abroad its renown, so that the little one of the desert, by a tender culture, by the skill of the horticulturist, and by the laws of transplanting, becomes a thousand, adorning our homes and sending a charm to the vision of those who pass our doors. To both of these kinds of men it is said, "Ascend." To the first the ascent means, not more false growth, but more solidity; not more show and form, but more reality and substance; not a larger pyramid, but a sounder base; and to the second, the "higher," is a call forward, from worth to renown, from an isolated beauty to public acknowledgment, from oneness to universality, from a secrecy in the desert to a force, beauty, and glory everywhere. Both are to advance; but the one must go backward first, and must make up for past deficiencies and for past slips, while the other, having a good foundation, is ordered simply with vigor to build upon it and to adorn it, that earth may be blessed and that Heaven may rejoice. The law of progress, without doubt, holds good in heaven; for we are not to suppose that perfection reaches us just as soon as we reach the celestial land. All actual sin, of course, departs; but we do not acquire at once all possible wisdom, a completed honor, a finished knowledge, and a thorough holiness. We are to grow as angels: we are to pass from one rank to another, on and ever on; and every new gain will be a fresh joy,—on, ever on, from angel to archangel, through billions of years,—never wearied of the flight, never gaining the summit, but always getting new strength and fresh joy and holy beauty.

Finally, my friends, the great lesson that we are to gather from our thoughts is this,—one that I always like to present,—that none of us are good enough, that all of us can be better, and that the very prayer, "O God, set us up on high," betokens that we are lower than we ought to be; and, therefore, there is no time, no reason, and no room for standing still. For the constant call of God, Jesus, the angels, and our own heart, is, Son or daughter, advance, go forward, look aloft, ascend, and mount, higher and higher, ever and forever.

"O God, set me up on high!"— set us all up higher!

Very soon we shall have nothing to do but to go from time to eternity into the higher places of the truest spiritual growth. "Nothing to do but to go." One uttered those words once. Perhaps you have all heard them or heard me repeat them before.

"NOTHING TO DO BUT TO GO."

"A wanderer I've been, and have travelled for years
   By the stage-coach, the steam-boat, the train.
I have known joyful meetings, have shed parting tears,
   With friends I might ne'er meet again.
And I've learned, let my farewells be joyous or sad,
   No haste or distraction to show,
But with baggage prechecked and with passage prepaid
   To have nothing to do but to go.

"The loiterer, when over the iron-clad track
   The train is heard coming apace,
For his ticket will clamor and urge for his check
   In a whirl of impatient distress.
Whilst others, more timeful, with undisturbed mien,
   Will composedly pace to and fro,
Or, quietly seated, will wait for the train,
   With nothing to do but to go.

"Oh! thus I have thought, when called to depart
   For the land whence we never return,
May we feel we are fully prepared for the start
   When the death-sounding note we discern.

With our ticket secured and our cares all at rest,
No disquieting thoughts may we know,
But, tranquilly waiting, be found at the last
With nothing to do but to go."

And, when we go, let us each utter the prayer, "O God, set us up on high!"— high in the way of duty, progress, and holiness, forever and ever.

XXIII.

THE COMMANDS OF GOD.

"Thus saith the Lord."— Ex. xi. 4.

CAN any one imagine any sentence of Scripture that is more imposing, comforting, commanding, beautiful, and suggestive than the one that we have chosen for our lesson at this sacred time?

Does not each one's experience, from birth to the present hour, acknowledge, reveal with eagerness, and proclaim with great unction the fact that all through life there has been a guiding voice, which has made clear, uplifting, and glorious to the consciousness the right way out of difficulty and the loyal, holy, and blessed means of attaining victory here and glory hereafter? We may all of us have disobeyed our higher intimations: we may have shut out all communication from above, muffled the ears of the soul, and chosen ourselves for guides, preferring to have our own way; yet we dare not deny that God has endeavored to help, bless, and save us during all our earthly pilgrimage. Every one of us knows full well that often, when beset by temptation, involved in perplexity, and darkened by trial, we have been startled, aroused, and comforted by a voice in the inner chambers of the heart, that articulated quite clearly, urgently, and eloquently, with unction, sublimity, and glory, "Thus saith the Lord." If we followed the direction, implicitly obeyed the message, and with alacrity marched on the appointed way, we have good reason to be grateful for the interference; and we are quite ready and very glad to acknowledge the wisdom, the mercy, and the comforting power of the speaker. But, if we have disobeyed the direction, mocked or scowled at its suggestions, and desired to be guided by our own short wisdom, dwarfed strength, and miserable guessing, then we have good reason to confess our folly, manifest our penitence, and return to the Guide who has been so long, foolishly, and terribly neglected.

Can we not all of us, in looking upon our past experience, trace the dividing line, the absolute crisis, and the guide-post in our history,— the point from which our present prosperity or our present distress can be clearly marked out?

How often we hear one exclaiming: "My whole life has been a mistake. I started wrong. I had every inducement to go one way, but my obstinacy drove me another way. Friends reasoned with me, my better judgment seconded their appeals; and yet my perverse will goaded me on to destruction"!

How many persons, even if they have not been seriously swamped in sin, have yet felt that their whole existence has been clouded by an early mistake,— simply because they entered the wrong door, took up the wrong instrument, went against the grain of their genius, and steered right in the face of "Thus saith the Lord"!

Then, again, how many hearing God speak, or thinking that he speaks, or sure that he must speak, interpret the voice, obey it, and hold it in high honor, although the career marked out, the duty enforced, the suffering commanded, the peril invoked, and the hardships of all kinds at hand are sure to come, are fearful to consider, and will be painful to endure! Yet these heroes — pale, it may be, in the face; trembling, perhaps, inwardly in the heart; thinking, too, of dear ones who are anxious — march forward, face all trouble, go through all difficulties, see thousands falling on the right and left, and yet are kept up and safely return to their home, with work done, with scars as trophies of fidelity to conviction, and with a record of honor that can never be wiped out. Our directions from Heaven are entirely personal: they are shaped according to our necessities, have especial reference to us, and, of course, fit and apply to nobody else. So each one of us has to study, not what the world says, not what our neighbors or our dearest friends say, but only what Almighty God tells us to think, do, and suffer. We are to listen for God's voice marking out our career; we are to seek for that, are to embrace that; and then we are cordially to give to it a prompt, a holy, and a faithful obedience. Faber speaks beautifully of the sweet will of God: —

> "I worship thee, sweet will of God,
>   And all thy ways adore;
> And every day I live I seem
>   To love thee more and more.
>
> "When obstacles and trials seem
>   Like prison-walls to be,
> I do the little I can do,
>   And leave the rest to thee.
>
> "I know not what it is to doubt,
>   My heart is ever gay.
> I run no risk; for, come what will,
>   Thou always hast thy way."

A great part of the sins that are prevalent in society to-day can be traced to the pernicious error that is so common amongst us all of listening for the voice of the multitude, and forgetting the inward voice that comes down from Heaven; that is, a good many people seem to prefer to lean upon arms of flesh rather than to rest patiently in the arms of God.

You and I, if we have read aright God's intention in our creation, if we understand in the least the teachings of the Bible, and if we have searched to any extent into the mysteries that encircle our being, must be aware that, as far as the formation of character is concerned, we are to get our inspiration, derive our strength, achieve our triumphs, and fight our battles mainly outside of human opinions, without any special regard to the verdict of those who are as frail as ourselves, and without looking for any chart save the chart that is written out in the great Book of God. How many are there who can solemnly, truthfully, and thankfully assert that their spirituality has never been twisted, their morality never been wrenched, their conscience never darkened, and their career never ordered by the direction of human beings as frail as themselves?

How many can say that their "Thus saith the Lord" has never received an alloy to its brightness, a tinge to its authority, a diminution of its power, and an abrasion of its glory by the voices of other dictators, such as "Thus saith the public," "Thus say the leading classes," and "Thus custom, expediency, worldly comfort, a good reputation, a splendid prosperity, and a desire for honors, dictate, urge, and command"? Again, there are many scenes in life that are constantly occurring where we can hardly utter a "Thus saith the Lord" without a shudder. Can any one visit any of our hospitals, and notice the multitudes of sufferers, the complexity of diseases, the varied ages and circumstances of the patients, the vast area of space filled with the wounded or the troubled, — at the same time bearing in mind the myriad ones far away whose souls are torn with anguish and whose hearts are convulsed with grief as they think of the absent and loved, — can any one thus look on these sights, and exclaim without any qualifications, "Thus saith the Lord"? Can any one scan a battle-field, looking at the ploughed earth, gazing at the crushed trees, beholding the image of man shattered, beasts of burden mutilated, stray cannon-balls, muskets that have fallen from palsied hands, swords that are to be grasped by their owners no more,— all the mêlée, the dishabille, and the débris which a war, like a vast conflagration, spreads around the crimson-stained ground,— and say, looking on both sides of the combatants, "Thus saith the Lord" to all engaged? Can any one enter a prison, and notice hundreds of convicts,— all punished for varied crimes, all sentenced for different terms; some placed in solitary confinement, others forced into the workshops; many so feeble as to be placed in the sick ward,— can one view these sights, then chant with an admirable composure, with an heroic serenity, and with a glorious hallelujah, "Thus saith the Lord"? No, no. Brethren, an everlasting no to such questions. For it is not obedience to Heaven that has brought calamity, suffering, and desolation upon the earth; for, if all God's children listened to the higher voice, none or but very little of the awful scenes around us would have happened, and crime would be a thing unknown.

It is because God's voice is not sought, heard, reverenced, obeyed, glorified, that strife is engendered, opposition created, warfare called forth, and force invoked; and always in every conflict there must be wrong somewhere, treachery at some point, disloyalty in some heart, and disorder, anarchy, and rebellion in some place. Although it has been said that very slight causes have created the great wars of the world, I say no,— an emphatic, earnest, heartfelt no; for, although the apparent cause may be in some cases but a trifle, the real cause is the decay of spirituality in some hearts, a turning from God in some direction, a forgetting of holiness, an impeachment of truth, and a denial of religion. For, if everybody in the world were a perfect saint, war would never be known; but, because oftentimes sin rises up, virtue has to rise up, in order to put the sin down.

Although there would be no battles if all were saints, yet, as all are not saints, ever since creation war, for various reasons, at unexpected times, and with great devastation, has had a hand in the building up of the world; and in a great many wars there has been a right side and a wrong side, so that those who have been willing to place themselves on the right side have been glad to leave home, ready to endure hardness, toil, and sacrifice, — ay, all prepared, perhaps, to lose mortal life for the sake of a noble principle. And such heroes have been inspired by the one great thought, "Thus saith the Lord."

Once more, as we gaze at all holy revolutions in Church or in State, we find that the nucleus of their growth rests mainly on a direct or a supposed revelation from Heaven.

The cross seen in the heavens by the Emperor Constantine, with the inscription that was embossed upon it, "By this conquer," is simply symbolic of an impressive truth; namely, that the basis of all great movements, the life of all mighty enterprises, and the charter and security for all success and all reputation must be of divine origin. Of every great reformer it is asked, and properly, too, Where is your commission? Then, unless the spiritual badge is shown, the people will not believe or follow. Even impostors, aware of this philosophical fact, in order to secure for their nefarious schemes an ultimate victory, borrow garments of light.

Notice, brethren, some of the great movements of the ages, and then see how they are brought about; and commence your search, if you please, among the heathen. In those dark times you will find that the household penates were constantly consulted ere any enterprise of weight was undertaken; and, What say the gods? was the first question of the Pagan. And then he did not care to go anywhere or to attempt to do anything until he knew what the gods did say, or, rather, what the priests said that they said.

Turn to the oldest Christian religion known, and then you will perceive that one great force resting in cathedral services and ceremonies, affiliating and attracting many persons to discipleship, is the constant reference to celestial things that the devout believer is taught each day to make. When he opens his eyes in the morning, there is a prayer for him to repeat; as he rises from his bed, bathes, dresses, goes to his meal, starts for his office,—ay, through every crevice of his day's duties,—there is a prayer provided. Thus are all temporal concerns covered by eternal realities, and thus God's light is thrown over all earthly darkness.

The old Church gave to the converted Pagan something that should prove a substitute for his household gods, and, instead of blocks of wood, offered him a book of prayers.

Again, when the Mother Church was divided, and when Protestantism was born out of her ranks, and when Martin Luther's name became emblazoned in history, the reason assigned for the revolution was wholly a spiritual one. Luther's creed was something like this: God wants faith; God wants every man to read his Bible; God wants prayers oral as well as prayers written, and he asks for less show and more substance.

Therefore, the seceders from the old Church went away, because they thought that they could get nearer to God. This was their honest plea, and it has been the honest plea of the thousand sects interlining the strata of Christianity ever since.

"Thus saith the Lord."

Ah! these words are emblazoned on the banner of every sect throughout the world; for each church claims to have received a special and a privileged hearing of the divine voice, and boasts of peculiar immunities that are not granted to others, and of rich intercommunications of gifts that are vouchsafed to them alone. But, thanks be to God, all these antagonistic denominations wish to bring about one grand result; namely, the culture, the salvation, and the coronation of the soul.

Once more, my friends, remember that many a weak or infamous design may be covered by a good name or by a bold front, and many a cruel deed has been varnished and labelled by the performer as an act of holiness; for it is a very comfortable subterfuge to throw the cloak of religion around our private, unholy, and selfish plans, while all the records of the past reveal specimens of this double dealing.

"For Christ's sake," so said the officers of the "Room of Agony," as they applied the rack and threw their victims into exquisite tortures; "for the Master's sake," so said the crusaders as they rushed into Asia with blood on their hearts and blood on their hands; "for the sake of religion," so have said many a king and many a queen, as they have signed the warrant for the burning of unbelievers or for the breaking of dissenters upon the wheel; "for the Redeemer's sake," so it is said to-day, when bigots rage, sects wrangle, hard blows are given, and wicked names are called, and thus the whole Christian world is thrown into dire confusion. Ah! how sad to think that human passion and human sin have borrowed divine robes, and have stolen celestial splendors only to hide an inward corruption and to make an apology for that which is so very base, startling, and cruel!

Hypocrisy, how contemptible! and cowardice, how abject! When we scan the character of our Master, thoroughly sifting the elements of which it is composed, we find that its rich beauty, solemn grandeur, magnificent power, and holy courage consisted in the constant heavenly reference that illuminated, sweetened, and encircled it.

He always followed the higher voice: it carried him into the temple, and sent him back with a gentle and a generous obedience to the home of his earthly guardians; it kept him fasting forty days and nights in the wilderness, exposed him to temptations, engirdled him with suffering, brought him to the cross, lifted him from the grave, and invested him with glory. Never any hesitation could be detected on the Master's part. As soon as he caught the breath of God, and when the command was issued, it was obeyed. He never questioned, but he performed; and it was not his pleasure to delay, but to march.

Oh, it was a glorious example of fidelity that he left for us, a very high standard for our admiration, and a majestic picture for our copy.

"Thus saith the Lord."

If we are sure of the direction, if we recognize without any reasonable doubts the voice, and if we are confident that we have a telephone connected with the altar of God, why then we must obey the communication,— no matter where it carries us; for God knows the way, has examined the pitfalls, gauged the precices, ipnoted down the mined roads, counted the broken bridges, is well aware of the impediments that are so thickly set against us on all sides, beholds as well as we do the deadly missiles flying through the air, and can manage — if he thinks proper— the shells, cannon-balls, and bayonet charges. But our duty is to go forward without dread, without hesitation, with a devout alacrity, and without a care as to the issue.

When God says, "Go," we are not to think of and see difficulties and dangers; or, if we cannot help thinking of them or seeing them, we are to rate them as nothing, face them without a shudder, and grapple with them with an earnest and a holy purpose, chanting all the while that glorious psalm, "The Lord is my shield and my buckler, of whom shall I be afraid?"

"We are told that in Cuba, during an insurrection, an Englishman's life was threatened, and soldiers were drawn up, ready to fire. The English consul and the American consul hurried to the spot, sprang from their carriage, and each wrapped their country's flag around the man, and, turning to the angry Spaniards, said, 'Now fire!' There was a hush. No one dared to fire upon flags that represented the two greatest powers in the world."

So, my friends, if God wraps around our souls the flag of heaven, we shall be safe anywhere and everywhere.

"Thus saith the Lord."

This is the motto, Christian friends, that I wish to see braided into your whole experience.

It is written in striking, golden, and burning letters upon the heavens. Oh, look and read it there, majestic in its grandeur!

It is ingrained upon the earth. Oh, trace it out with your illuminated genius, and see how each letter of it is irradiated with splendor! May it be imbedded, too, in your thoughts, cut deep into your hearts, render melodious all your deeds! And then, whether you live or die, enjoy or suffer, are full or are empty, are surrounded by friends or are flanked by enemies, it will be a matter of but very little concern to you; for, come what may, you are armed, counselled, cheered, certainly safe, and really victorious, for all the angels of heaven are on your side.

XXIV.

THE BREVITY OF LIFE.

"Knoweth that he hath but a short time."— Rev. xii. 12.

NO more true, striking, solemn, and electric words were ever spoken; and yet probably no truth is ever more put out of sight, speedily dismissed, and thoroughly ignored than that which sets forth the fleetness of time.

We admit the fact with our lips, but we deny the reality in our lives; we approve of the sentiment, but very seldom in our experience do we make that sentiment blossom into a sacrament; and we are apt to live as if there were time enough, and we squander the hours as if there were plenty of hours to spare. So that, when the day of our death shall come, we shall be very much disturbed because our career is cut off so soon; and we are dismissed with plans half finished and with work half done.

We leave till to-morrow what ought to be done to-day, as if to-morrow had been promised to us beyond the quiver of a doubt; and the old saying is very correct that "every man thinks every man mortal except himself." Although death hovers around us in all shapes, although the cemetery is thoroughly peopled and friends and neighbors are disappearing all the time; yet, somehow, each one of us feels secure, as if a higher voice had said, "It shall not come nigh thee." Of course, it is not expected of us that we shall continually moan over the brevity of our earthly being. God does not wish that his children should always be cast down, dismayed, and disheartened. The mind would break if it were strained all the time on one note. Health would give way if the brain were forever shadowed; and we might as well live inside of a tomb as to be gazing at a tomb forever. And yet sometimes — ay, often — the soul needs to come into vital contact with the sad, sharp, and changing side of life; and it must, for its own good, peace, and true growth, ponder very frequently over the shifting days, hours, and years, for thus is energy braced, devotion roused, a mighty work accomplished, and thus do we conquer sloth, fear, and infidelity, and rise into the serene atmosphere of faith, hope, devotion, and good will. "Knoweth he hath a short time." Well, if the time be short for all of us, let us look up for light, march to our duty with an illuminated mind and a transfigured soul, and lift our burdens easily, make them a constant benediction, and convert them from darkness into a marvellous light. The longest life is short; and even threescore years and ten soon pass away, so that those who are aged speak of their life as a dream. But the average years of life, my friends, are only thirty; and how quickly those thirty years fade out of sight! For we are hardly born into one world ere we are summoned into another kingdom. Life and death are all the time struggling together for a blessed reconciliation, and the march from the cradle to the grave has to be taken with lightning speed. Consider how much of our being is taken up with getting ready to live, and how much is smothered by sleep. Think of the years that are used merely for the support of physical wants. Count the time when you are learning how to think, feel, and grow. See how often the blossoms are nipped, and how they cover the ground with a snowy shroud. And look even at the flowers and the fruit, how transitory their glory; "for they are soon cut off, and fly away." The brute, by instinct, springs into maturity quickly; but man is a plant of a slow growth, and he develops inch by inch, climbs the ladder of progress round by round, and goes step by step towards eternity. When we think of the slow opening of conscience, the tardy steps of judgment, the dilatory advance of reason, the measured tread of a well-furnished and a brilliantly lighted and a gloriously perfumed imagination, the solemn, prolonged, and wearing advance of burning ideas, then we exclaim, Oh, where is the opportunity for man, and how can he go forward? For he will die before he is able to begin, and by the time that he is ready to live the summons for his retreat will appear. His army will be collected, his weapons purchased and delivered, his powder distributed, the order of battle will be planned, and then, just as the time comes to act, a higher Power will withdraw his commission, revoke his authority, and call him to another command. Just as he wants to go forward, and while he can do so with apparent honor, he will be ordered away; and then all will cry out, Oh, what a pity, what a sacrifice, and what an untimely call! I declare, as I look upon the uncertainties of life, the hasty thought will sometimes come up, Why was man created, what good can he accomplish, and is not existence a terrible mistake? Ah! my friends, a great deal is accomplished, notwithstanding the brevity of the days; and it is really astonishing how much can be done by an earnest, devout, and holy spirit. And some names are graven deeply in history, because their owners were determined to grasp time, and were resolved to make it pay a ransom for its celerity and a premium on its speed.

"Oh, time!" they have virtually said, "you may be short; but you shall be sweet; you may love to run, but you shall drop fragrance as you go; and you may not give us many chances, but every chance that you do give to us shall be loaded with opportunities, covered with splendors, and shall yield a rich, an attractive, and a holy harvest. Oh, time! you may be without mercy, you may strike hard, you may strike deep, and you may attempt to trip us up in an unfortunate moment; but we will make you change your tune, reverse your tactics, ground your arms, and surrender unconditionally to our determined will; and you shall be anointed with our good resolutions, enriched, sanctified, and uplifted by our earnest prayers, hallowed, glorified, and sweetened by our holy deeds; and, like an Æolian harp, when the breath of our consecrated will touches you, you shall waft sweet music, warble heavenly harmonies, and send a breeze of glory into the ears of all who care to listen; while angels shall hear the melody with a thrill of delight. And you shall become our steward, ambassador, friend, brother; and we will crown you with garlands, while all your ways shall be ways of pleasantness and all your paths shall be paths of peace.

This is taking time, according to the ancient proverb, by the forelock; and this is the turning of its mission from that of a fiend to that of an angel.

Again, a great deal is accomplished in this world, not by any one man, but by the aggregate of men. Of course, men die, but the race lives; and so fresh hands take up the work that departed ones leave. And thus everything that we do tells, nothing is lost, one age helps another, and all men are bound in cordial harmony by a golden chain, from Adam's day till now; and thus, while life is important, no one life is especially so. And thus, when a great or a good man drops out of sight, we are not of necessity thrown into inextricable confusion, nor forced into incurable despair, nor left entirely deserted. And thus the world goes on, no matter what happens to individuals; for nothing can stay the march of improvement, nor the triumphal advance of right, nor God's eternal laws.

Men may die, but principles live; and time for any one person may be short, but all time is adequately long, will be nobly consecrated, and shall have a blessed fruitage.

God, in the creation of the world and in the making of man, did not create and did not make a mistake; for he knew the value of the soul and the worth of the body, — how long they ought to be in partnership, and when they should separate and lose their relative value. And he never created one man to do everything, and it is but a straw that each one of us can lift; and, if we all lift our straw, then will all things be full of harmony, holiness, and glory. Our work is simple, but grand, short, but sublime; and we are not to complain of it and to crave more time for the accomplishing of it, but we are to do it, and to do it cheerfully, beautifully, and thoroughly, with a right, and with a righteous spirit. The time may be short; but it is long enough for what we have to do, and plenty long enough for the development of our characters into all that God would have us to be.

Let us polish our life off, then, with care, adorn it with skill, set it in spiritual diamonds, and make it sparkle forever and ever. The time is long enough for us, through our patience, purity, and consistent holiness, to get our name written in the "Lamb's Book of Life"; and may our names be written there in bright, large, and glorious letters, and labelled as those who are faithful, persistent, patient, and pure, and as those who care only to make earth the stepping-stone to heaven, the outer portal that leads to the celestial gate, and the door that opens into the chambers of our God. Spiritually, we seem to forget how short are our days of discipline; and we postpone our penitence, consecration, and renewal, as if the future were entirely subject to our command,— just as if we had a lease of life, with the privilege of renewing it.

Time enough, we think, for us to attend to our souls after we have cared for the mind and the body: we will be good just before we die, and then we will do the whole work up at once. For we are too busy to be good now; but by and by, when our houses are built, our stables are full, our bank account is large, and we have retired from the bustle of the market, then we will turn over a new leaf, and turn it over very thoroughly. And those looking at us shall say that we are changed,— thoroughly changed for the better. And so we go on, nine out of ten, dropping into the grave before the time of rest, improvement, and growth arrives. And so, too, with those to whom a period of relief comes: it is hardly ever a renovation; for habit has so crisped the mind, enfeebled the heart, and weakened the hand that there is no disposition to change, while the loiterers prefer to go on in the old way. What is worth doing at any time is worth doing now.

The future that we expect may never come; and,

if it should come, every delay in goodness always brings about a loss. And why should we not be good now, why should we lose so many years of keen joy, real delight, solid comfort; and why should we waste in terrible unrest so many precious days? Suppose we do become saints just before we pass from the earth. Will our late discipleship compensate for the wrecks that we have made of the greater part of our existence; and will a few roses make up for so many thistles? Ah! we are wofully short-sighted when we come to deal with our souls; and, however massive may have been our intellect in everything else, in this one great thing we are apt to be very idiotic. In fact, if we governed trade as we govern the heart, trouble, danger, and ruin would soon be our portion, and a perfect chaos would fall upon all mercantile pursuits. If we carry the same energy, enthusiasm, devotion, and affection into the culture of our souls that we carry every day into the pursuit of our daily calling, we shall soon become what God would have us to be. We have but a short time: let us then do the best that we can, for we cannot do too much; and, although we work every minute, we shall still be unfinished, unfurnished, and terribly lacking. The completion of character is a duty that grows larger and much larger the more faithfully it is greeted; and it grows with our growth, expands with our efforts, forms new heights as the old ones are scaled.

Its law is ever on and up. It is never satisfied with what is accomplished, and always calls for more;

and, however good we may be, we are far below the true mark, and we must still "press forward to our high calling in Christ Jesus the Lord."

Ah! my friends, in the face of the words of the text, contrary to the apostolic seeming statement, and somehow as a paradox after what I have already said, I would declare that time is not short, because life and time merge into eternity. Grand, solemn, and majestic thought! And are we prepared for the sublime reconciliation, the heavenly marriage, and the wonderful apocalypse? Ah! these hours are invested with a sacred privilege, clothed with a fresh power, irradiated with a holy lustre, since we know that they cannot decay, since the chains and the bolts are taken off from them, and since they leap, career, and bound into the gulf of Infinity. Our thoughts now are wonderfully important, our habits must be strictly scanned, our deeds have a meaning they never had before; for there is an echo beyond the grave, there is a reverberation like the sound of a deep-toned bell through endless ages; and what we do in time is to have a resurrection in eternity.

Let us look well, then, to our ways, and crowd every second with glory; and let the influence that goes from us be constantly pure, serene, golden. And then those who gaze at us shall know that our eyes are upon the "pearly gates," that we have seen the pure white throne, and that we are longing for the new name that is given only to those whom the Lord approves; and let us make our life like a great organ, whose varied pipes celestial artists carve, whose different notes none but angel fingers touch, and out of which shall come harmonies that sanctify, elevate, and inspire all souls. As a proof how time on earth can be both short and long, let us look at Jesus Christ; and then we shall see how much he made of three years. For in that space he overturned the world.

Old systems, that thousands of years had fortified and strengthened, crumbled to pieces or were shaken to their very centre, and seeds of truth that never before could find soil enough for moisture or for nourishment, by his blessed aid and sweet inspiration found root and got solid growth. And he gave freedom to ideas, depth, wealth, and joy to affections, and an eternal echo to deeds. He robed pain in celestial garments, clothed all earthly discipline in a vesture of heavenly white, and robbed death of its terror and name, making the grave a garden; and the future, so dreary and uncertain and every way so uninviting, he filled with a glory, arched with a benediction, and fused with a splendor that was meant to dazzle all eyes and subdue, convince, and glorify all hearts.

Yes, it was three years' ceaseless work, from the time that the sun leaped into its morning brightness till at eventide the same bright orb went to sleep in golden robes.

He scattered his favors by word, by deed, and by look, from the moment that he issued from his banishment and victory in the wilderness till he cried from the cross those terribly significant yet somehow suggestive, inspiring, and majestic words, "It is finished."

He never allowed himself to be overcome by fatigue, was always ready to do the Father's will; and, certainly, he, best of all, has taught us the value of the hours; has clearly proved how much radiance may leap out of even the briefest life; has made it clear that it is the quality of one's existence that makes it long, and not the quantity of it; and has taught that length of days is not to be desired for a moment except so far as we can make our days fragrant, pure, and beautiful. And let us heed these great, glorious, and soul-stirring lessons.

Bickersteth says: —

"Our years are like the shadows
  O'er sunny hills that fly,
Or grasses in the meadows,
  That blossom but to die,
A sleep, a dream, a story
  By strangers quickly told,
An unremaining glory
  Of things that soon are old.

"O Thou, who canst not slumber,
  Whose light grows never pale,
Teach us aright to number
  Our years before they fail.
On us thy mercy lighten,
  On us thy goodness rest,
And let thy spirit brighten
  The hearts thyself hath blessed."

XXV.

A POSTPONED CONCLUSION.

"But the end is not yet." — ST. MATT. xxiv. 6.

I THINK that we derive a peculiar satisfaction when we can say of anything that it is finished; and we are still more happy, comforted, and strengthened when we can say it is well finished. The bad man likes to have his work done, well over, and the profits gathered, ere conscience has lashed him into remorse, remorse has driven him to penitence, and penitence has stopped him midway on the road to great gains; but, above all, and with a keen relish, the good man views with delight a noble duty finished, a holy contest ended, truth triumphant, philanthropy crowned, and everything beautifully and grandly and gloriously rounded off. Then the toil endured, the rebuffs greeted, the patience taxed, and all the wear and tear undergone in the execution of the work are no more considered, and are rated as trifles when compared with the magnificent achievement which is their holy fruitage, beautiful coronation, and sublime compensation.

Review your own life, each one; and then find out if the truth which I have stated be not indorsed by your experience. I will question you only in regard to your good works. Where you have given yourself up to the service of others, to the establishment of right, and to the glorification of souls,— no matter how long our service, nor how tedious our labor, and no matter if your strength, temper, and faith almost gave out,— yet, when it was done and finished exactly as you desired, have you cared for the time, struggle, life, and health that you have consecrated, have you estimated those things in the least, and are they not wiped out of consideration by your joy, peace, and the holy echoes in your heart?

Are they not cancelled from your mind by the gratitude of those whom you have helped? and are they not viewed as of no account as you lift up your thanksgivings unto God, from whose gracious love the victory came? Assure me of success in any good thing that I may undertake, and then what do I care for the price, suffering, and penalty? And, though I know that I must lose my sight, or my health, or my mind, or my life, what do I care, and why should I care, as long as I accomplish my holy designs, and as long as Heaven smiles upon my labors?

God himself, it is said in Holy Writ, "blessed the seventh day, and hallowed it," because on that day the early creation was completed.

He viewed heaven, earth, light, darkness, dry land, water, day, night, grass, herb, tree, stars, sun, moon, fowls, whales, and all living creatures as a good creation, a well-finished work, and something at which it was right for him to rejoice. We have the highest authority, then, for sacred delight, when we think that we have done well, when we feel that our work is rightly finished, and when we have carried out a good design.

Again, Christ on the cross, in that terrible hour of agony when he surveyed a world convulsed by sin, counted up the certain triumphs of the religion that he had inaugurated, was sure that the seed which he had dropped into such unpromising ground would fertilize the soil on which it fell, and would become wonderfully productive, and could see the certain advance of Christianity in spite of all the efforts that would be made to defeat it. Christ himself joyfully exclaimed, "It is finished."

Was there not a glow of satisfaction about him in the thought that his work was done, and must not this thought have been a comfort to him in his dying hour, and did not the angels catch those words up,— "It is finished!"— chanting them with their grand, beautiful, and glorious hosannas?

But, my friends, I repeat, whether our work be good or bad, we are glad when it is over. We carry this feeling with us also as we review past ages. However much we may like to study their history, sift their records, probe their great men, admire their achievements, and revel among their splendors, we are nevertheless very glad that these ages are over, that they are never to be repeated, and that we are left unimpeded, so that we can make the days in which we live peculiarly our own,— shaped by our ideas, words, and deeds.

I will admit that many speak of the good old times, of the virtues of their ancestors, and of the degeneracy of the present age, while they pretend that they wish that they were back again where their fathers were; but they forget, as they speak, that, in order to go back, they must wipe out of existence the telegraph, railroad, steamship, telephone, the advance of letters, the triumphs of the arts and sciences, and the thousand improvements that have made life so important, time so valuable, and the days so grand. I know that many speak of the good old times, but they mean nothing by what they say: they are dreaming; and, if you persistently address them with questions, drive them to definite statements, strong arguments, and cogent logic, they will break right down, will acknowledge that they are in the wrong, and will own that all they want of past times is the good, not the bad, and that all that they wish to lose of the present is the bad, and not the good; that is, all that such wish is to have society perfect, men angels, and earth heaven, but for a simple exchange — present for past — they would not for a moment consent. Again, some people talk in a complaining way of the present, with profuse compliments for the past,— not because they know anything of history, for, as a general rule, such persons are the most profoundly ignorant about past ages; but they speak in this way because they are never satisfied with anything, are usually and always uneasy, and want just what they do not possess.

They would have made the same complaint a hundred years ago,— nay, a thousand years ago: ay, they would have said the same in the days of Genesis; while our chief hope is that, if they be allowed at last to enter heaven, their natures may be changed, sweetened, and glorified, or else there they will be unhappy, and will be longing for the earth, their bodies, and the good old times.

Again, as we look back upon our own lives, we do not wish to live them over again.

I know that many say, "Oh that I could be a child once more!" But ask them what they mean, and they will reply that they want to carry back into their new childhood all the experience that they have gained up to the period in which they have lived; that is, they want to have the body of a child and the mind of a man. But this they know is an utter impossibility. No: we do not want to go back to infancy again, in order that we may make the same mistakes when we are growing up that we have already made; for perhaps with the new chance we should fail still more. And we should be afraid to run the risk, and we should prefer to go to God as we are than as we might be under another trial of life. But, my friends, although we like the end of everything, think that the end is better than the beginning, and do not want to repeat past work or to call back former ages, yet the words of our text say, "The end is not yet"; and true Christianity affirms also that there is really no end to anything, and that what appears to be so is simply a delusion.

I suppose that many of us are thinking that on the last Sabbath of the year the year is nearly gone; and so it is about gone, if we refer to months, weeks, days, and minutes. Yes, about departed are its opportunities, nearly disappeared its responsibilities, and almost closed its record.

Yes, many a keen joy has vanished, many a bitter sorrow has faded away, and the panorama of events cannot again pass before our eyes.

The last Sunday in the year is always one of peculiar solemnity; for into it are gathered so many precious memories, so many holy hopes, so many good resolutions, and so much deep penitence. For we seem to be standing on sacred ground, and we hear God's voice calling us to account.

We began the year, it may be, with the solemn desire to lead a better life than ever before; and we were determined, both at home and abroad, to be holier men or braver women or more obedient children.

We confessed that we ought to turn over a new leaf, act from higher principles, and that in many of our deeds we had been very hasty, inconsiderate, and impious,— had not thought enough of God, Jesus, heaven, earth, our fellow-men, and ourselves.

As we felt this personal deficiency, we were determined that coming days should find us more faithful, sincere, pure, moral, and religious. And these were good resolutions, noble thoughts, holy desires; and God heard them, I doubt not, with joy, and the holy angels chanted, it may be, their delight. But have we kept such promises? Have we consecrated these good thoughts, and are we very much advanced in Christian manliness, and have we good reason to be religiously satisfied as we gaze at fifty-two weeks closed up, passed by, done with forever? Have we learned to govern our temper, appetites, and desires? Is our word now as good as our bond, are our prayers more frequent, holy, and sincere, and have we grown into noble specimens of God's workmanship,— that of us it may be said "we are not far from the kingdom of heaven"; ay, even more than this, that we are even treading the outer courts of the celestial city? Ah! to our shame be it said that none of us can utter a hearty, holy, and truthful Amen to these searching questions. We kept our vows, it may be, hardly a week. They were early broken, formed again, and again violated; and all the year has been spent in turning over the new leaf, which, after all, seems to be nothing but the old leaf stereotyped. And here we are year after year repeating the same promises, and asking Heaven to smile upon, bless, and hallow our resolutions.

But is it mummery, after all? Do we not mean what we say? And, when we say that we are sorry that past years have not been more profitable, and when we promise that coming ones shall bear a better record of us, are we not perfectly sincere, contrite, and earnest? We may fail in our design the very first day of the new year; but, still, are we not sincere?

I think that we do mean to be better, and that we are grieved because we have been so weak, and that our failure arises from the fact that we trust too much to our own strength and rely too much on our own right arm.

Let us go into all coming days with our own strength, but with a portion of God's strength also,— a strength so much better than ours, and without which ours will be as nothing, a mere beating of the air.

Oh, let us kneel before Almighty God in the privacy of our chambers, and confess that we leave all our old years with sad misgivings as to their testimony concerning our worth, and that we know on many of their days are black marks against our names; and let us own that we earnestly look now for pardon, peace, joy, and for a grace that shall be sufficient for us in all approaching hours.

Ah! these wrestlings with God in private bring thousands and tens of thousands of angels to our help, and clothe us with a celestial armor that cannot be destroyed.

"The end is not yet."

Thanks be to God that we have a further opportunity for amendment, that we have another chance for retrieving our character, and that the mortgage against our souls has not been foreclosed! Farewell to all time that has passed! Let us say to the years, We have been friends together: you have shared with us our joys and sorrows, have seen our eyes beam with gladness at unexpected pleasures and dim with tears when sorrows came uninvited; and in all the vicissitudes of our experience you have been present, watching, helping, and consecrating. Oh, forgive us that we have so little prized and so little hallowed your fellowship, that we have stained your heart with our sins, and speak charitably of us as you appear before God with the tablet that bears the ineffaceable account of our doings, and tell to all sister years that are coming to take your place that we will endeavor to treat them better, and that we hope they may treat us with a holy, blessed, and uplifting gentleness.

Farewell once more to the passing years! They keep going away, as they must, with our broken vows, unholy deeds, and cold devotions. But God grant, with our sincere penitence, with the certain assurance of our future well-being, and with a kindling hope, that, by the mercy of God, we may stand forgiven at the great altar of Heaven!

www.ingramcontent.com/pod-product-compliance
Lightning Source LLC
Chambersburg PA
CBHW031945230426
43672CB00010B/2055